THE NANTUCKET TABLE

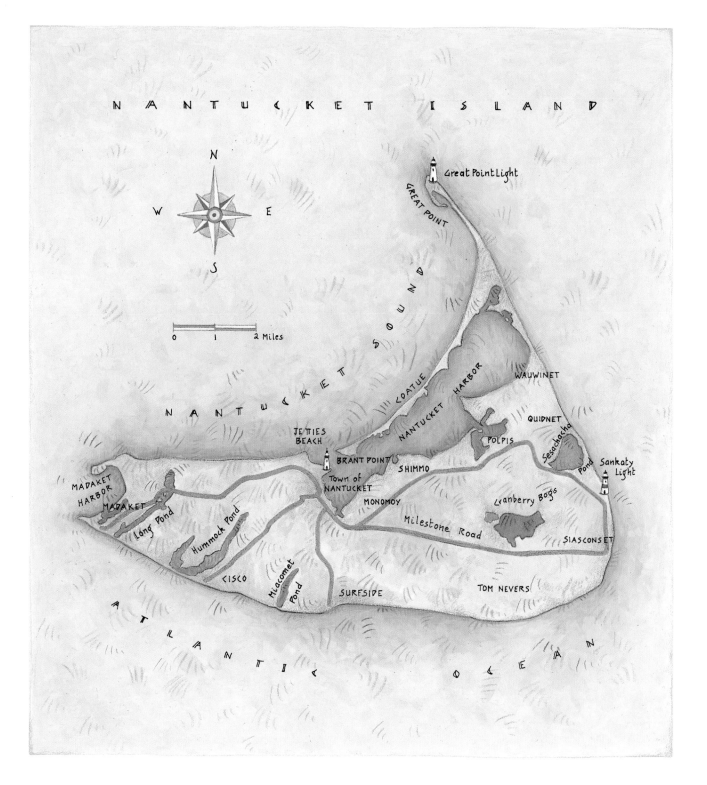

THE NANTUCKET TABLE

Susan Simon

PHOTOGRAPHS BY TOM ECKERLE

CHRONICLE BOOKS
SAN FRANCISCO

For Laura,
The garden looks fabulous!

First Chronicle Books paperback edition, published in 2004.

ISBN 0-8118-4438-2

The Library of Congress has cataloged the previous edition as follows:

Simon, Susan.
        The Nantucket table/by Susan Simon; photographs by Tom Eckerle.
              p.   cm.
        Includes index.
        ISBN 0-8118-1472-6
              1. Cookery, American—New England style.   2. Cookery—
Massachusetts—Nantucket.   I. Title.
        TX715.2.N48S54   1998
        641.5974—dc21   97–30797
                                                              CIP

Manufactured in China.

Designed by Howard Klein

Map of Nantucket © 1998 by Françoise Humbert

Distributed in Canada by Raincoast Books
9050 Shaughnessy Street
Vancouver, British Columbia V6P 6E5

10 9 8 7 6 5 4 3 2 1

Chronicle Books LLC
85 Second Street
San Francisco, California 94105

www.chroniclebooks.com

ACKNOWLEDGMENTS

To my agent, Marian Young, who has the courage of her motto, "clients for life, friends for life," staying with me until the idea for this book was made publishing presentable—and then found the perfect editor in Bill LeBlond, whose vision about Nantucket's table was right on course with mine. To Bill's associates and assistants at Chronicle Books: Leslie Jonath, Sarah Putman, and Judith Dunham, who eased the editing process with precision and grace; Laura Lovett, who guided the book's design; and an old friend, Howard Klein, whose spacious design captures the atmosphere of Nantucket.

To say that the book looks this way as the result of a collaboration would be putting it mildly. To Tom Eckerle, who took the extraordinary photographs, and to Ceci Gallini, who wore many hats during our production: prop stylist, photographer's assistant, and Mamma to Kate and Matteo Eckerle.

To the friends and acquaintances long-standing and brand-new on Nantucket, who opened their homes, lent props, donated food and wine, and generously supplied information: Dan and Nancy Bills of The Lion's Paw; Jim Lentowski, Janet Jones, and Rick Blair of The Nantucket Conservation Foundation, Dennis Metcalfe of Nantucket Moorings, Melissa and Dean Long of Nantucket Vineyard; Glidden's Island Seafood; Joyce and Michel Berruet of L'Ile de France; Steve Slosek of Moors End Farm; Dorothy Bartlett of Bartlett's Ocean View Farm; Chin Manasmontri, Pat Tyler, and Dan Ferrare of the West Creek Cafe; Peter and Thea Kaizer; Gwen Gaillard, Steve Bender, Mimi Beman, Nat Philbrick, Sarah Mellin, and Dan Marino; Lynda Hoff and Tim Mellin; John and Dinah Mellin; Gilbert Mellin; Ann Hanson; Mina Manner; Missy and Lee Isgur; Karen Pelrine and Douglas Pinney; Lee Gaw; Kathryn and Roy Clauss; Samantha Rand; Tony Yates; Andy Roberts; and Kenny Duce.

To my mainland friends who lent props, ideas, and advice: John Derian, Ilona Granet, Ellen Hanson of Altfield, Eden Ross Lipson, Charles Mohacey, Tom Pearson, Sandra Oliver, Susan Kirby, and Gay Jordan, who introduced me to chicken-almond rounds.

To Roy Finamore, friend and contributor, instigator and accomplice.

To Laura Simon and Jimmy Gross for the big gifts of understanding, patience, and support, not diminished by the other gifts that meant so much to this production: off-season shelter, fresh vegetables, flowers, eggs, and honey.

To Musetta, constant muse.

To all of you, from my heart, thank you.

CONTENTS

Intoxicated by the heady fragrance of rugosa roses and the pungent, nose-curling salt air, I stumbled down the gangplank of the ferry S.S. *Nobska* and set foot on Nantucket for the first time, fourth of July weekend, 1960. My first visit to the Island, twenty-six miles out to sea, off Cape Cod, was only a long weekend. At the Jetties Beach I walked for what seemed like miles to find water deep enough to swim in, and at Surfside Beach I recklessly rode the waves. Then I went sightseeing, by bike, past silver-shingled houses, blowsy pastel gardens, and rugged, scrubby moors until my breath was taken away. That weekend, thirty-eight years

ago, my late mother, my sister, and I began the adventures that became our new history. After that first weekend, my Nantucket time was limited to school summer vacations when I worked at various jobs from chambermaid to sketch artist. When I moved to Italy in 1965 and

Nantucket was really far away, I returned to the Island only for an occasional holiday visit. In 1974 I came to Nantucket and stayed for a full six years.

My sister, Laura, and her husband, Jim Gross, had decided that same year to make Nantucket their primary residence. During the six years that I lived on the Island, I worked every winter as a commercial scalloper with Jimmy. My mother, Hilda, had also decided to call Nantucket home in 1974 and opened a fabric shop on Main Street called "The Calico Whale." She subconsciously (I think) continued a tradition begun over one hundred years previously by the resourceful wives of whalers-out-to-sea who stocked their Petticoat Lane (now Centre Street) shops with fine dry goods and fancy pantry items, and offered for sale at her shop the finest natural fiber fabrics, notions, and ribbons.

Just over a century earlier, on the fourth of July weekend 1852, Herman Melville came to Nantucket for the first time, a full year after the publication of *Moby Dick*, in which he wrote this oft-repeated description of the Island: "Nantucket! Take out your map and look at it. See what a real corner of the world it occupies; how it stands there, away off shore, more lonely than the Eddystone lighthouse. Look at it—a mere hillock, and elbow of sand; all beach, without a background." Upon his arrival he was slightly taken aback to find the Island almost deserted. Most of the inhabitants had gone across the sound to Hyannis to enjoy the Independence Day celebrations and watch the fireworks display. What he did see, however, affected him tremendously.

In a later conversation with his friend Nathaniel Hawthorne, Melville spoke of the extraordinary ways the women of Nantucket had become the superintendents of the Island while their husbands were away whaling. These enterprising women had their Petticoat Lane businesses in town and also worked the family farms to their full commercial possibilities. The harvests provisioned many whaling ships and in fact often surpassed in profits the earnings of the whaler husbands.

The women were a link in the history of an occupation that is as old as the human habitation of Nantucket. The Native Americans were farmers, as were the settlers, who cultivated corn, wheat, barley, and rye. Most of the farms, the majority of which were in Polpis, also raised cattle, hogs, and sheep.

Sheepherding was a natural industry for the Island, far from the

intrusion of the enemy of the gentle beast, the wolf. It gave Nantucket its economic base until it was overshadowed by whaling. Because whaling was so great a source of revenue, throughout the late eighteenth century and into the middle of the nineteenth century, the Island was considered the wealthiest port in the world.

Unfortunately, the pursuit of whales for profit began to decline slowly following the Great Fire of 1846, which destroyed more than a third of Nantucket town, including the wharves. But the real cause of the demise was the discovery in 1859, in the fields of western Pennsylvania, of petroleum. By the 1880s the dearth of work caused Nantucket's population to decrease as Islanders embarked for the mainland to search out employment and a new life. Those who remained returned to farming. Though the waters surrounding the Island teemed with fish, the industry devoted to catching them had died out long ago. According to Clint Andrews in his informative book *Fishing around Nantucket*, "Although the earliest settlers tried to give codfishing priority in development, the exceptionally

favorable circumstances for whaling overtook it immediately. Whaling products were more valuable than fish, and whaling required more highly skilled seamen and in greater numbers than fishing. This was just what Nantucket had to offer, but the Island did not have the manpower to supply the requirements of both industries."

The Island farms were more subsistence than income producing. Fortunately, at more or less the same time, the muscle of the bay scallop was discovered to be not only highly edible but also much prized and sought after by New York City's fancy restaurants. This allowed the farmers to spend the warm summer months growing food to feed their families for the year and then to spend the colder months fishing in the harbor for scallops, which could be sold for export. To this day, scalloping is the Nantucket cold-weather industry, enriching the coffers of many Islanders.

The dairy industry was a business important to Nantucket's daily life, but its future wasn't as secure as that of scalloping. Out in the Shimmo Valley, Seth Clisby had a little dairy farm. His original barn is still standing on what is now the Slosek's Moors End Farm. When

Stanley Slosek bought the "Clisby Place" in 1957, there had been a few owners between him and Seth, all of whom had devoted the property to dairy farming. Stanley ran the farm as the Nantucket Dairy for as long as there was a market for fresh local milk. In 1968, without the support that he needed to continue, Stanley closed the dairy. Stanley's son Steve, and his wife, Sue, started vegetable gardening on the property and began to sell their produce from a wheelbarrow situated at the edge of the Polpis Road. Word spread about the quality of their vegetables and that it was a convenient shopping location for the population of Nantucket's east and north ends. At the stand, now on the far side of the farm's parking lot, customers can choose from vegetables picked exactly when ripe, including Moors End's legendary sweet corn.

On the other side of the Island, at Cisco, Bartlett's Ocean View Farm cultivates over one hundred acres that supply Islanders with, among other things, the same tomatoes with which Phil Bartlett started vegetable gardening. From its beginnings, the farm had been a dairy, passed from one generation of Bartletts to another. New laws in the late 1940s required farms to put in pasteurization plants, and Phil's father, the celebrated "June," gave up cows and tried sheepherding, Nantucket's original industry. At about the same time, Phil was working at Ed Gardner's Mt. Vernon Farm (no longer in production) just down the road from Bartlett's. Phil's passion was growing tomatoes, and with encouraging advice from Ed, he convinced his grandmother to let him use her front yard, far from the grazing sheep, to try a tomato planting. The tomatoes flourished, which was fortuitous, because the sheep didn't fare as well. Now, every spring, summer, and fall, Bartlett's delightfully colorful and inviting truck stand, parked at the corner of Main and Federal Streets, sells the freshest produce and inspires legions of artists to reproduce the sight.

There's no question that the enormous success of these farms is due in no small way to the transformation of Nantucket from turn-of-the-century summer place to sleepy vacation spot to world-class resort. While Moors End Farm and Bartlett's Ocean View Farm were coming into their own as major suppliers of fresh vegetables to Nantucket's citizens and restaurants, I was off traveling in other parts of the world, coming into my own. My base of operations was Italy, where I came to study painting, and from there I branched out, unknowingly gathering the information that I would later need to create this book.

I traveled by train to England, then to Spain, and from there to Sicily. The outdoor markets of the cities, towns, and villages that I visited, with their piles and stacks of fresh fruits and vegetables, cheeses, fish, game, and poultry, always drew my attention and fascinated me. I was impressed with the way the shoppers would be in the market every day to procure the freshest ingredients to make simple and tasty meals. I stayed in Morocco for a month; spent a summer in Sardinia; drove through Scotland, Czechoslovakia, Austria, France, and Spain again; lived for a year in the Seychelles Islands; and ate and drank my way through Italy from top to bottom and then back up again.

Filled with memories and ideas, I returned to the States in 1974 and landed on Nantucket. I came to the Island because it was now home. It was where my parents were and it was where my sister, Laura, and Jimmy were. I continued my pattern of employment begun so long ago and juggled jobs from season to season. The only sure employment was that on November first every year, Jimmy and I would board *Gale Winds*, steer her out into the harbor, drop the first dredge, and begin to catch the most prestigious scallop in the world, the Nantucket bay.

I found Nantucket life very seductive, but I felt unsettled. In 1981 I moved to New York City and opened a catering business. At every available opportunity, and always in the summer, I would return to the Island. In 1994 I decided that I wanted to stay for a greater stretch of time than I usually had. I rented a little shingled cottage in Quidnet, on the Island's east end. The cottage, called "Airdrie," built in the 1920s, sits in a clearing surrounded by scrub oaks, bayberry bushes, and wild viburnum. Trellises cover the façade, and the roses that climb over the white latticework appear to be as old as the structure itself. You can hear the slosh and swoosh of the ocean, which is about five hundred yards away. For me, this is quintessential Nantucket: elegant, relaxed, and cozy. What better setting to write a book about food that is also elegant, easy, and true to the offerings of the seasons.

This collection of recipes is not just for special occasions, but mostly just plain, honest, fresh, and interesting, unaffected food. In writing this book, I was lucky to have available for recipe creating and testing the good assortment of vegetables offered for sale by Bartlett's and Moors End farms, along with the salty selections found in the local fish markets. Throughout the chapters you will find a central theme. While the main ingredients of each recipe are Nantucket fresh, the trademark style of my food is diversity. Drawing on the cuisines that are a direct result of my traveling, I add simple ingredients to the main one to create the Nantucket table. Fresh salmon spread with a paste of cilantro and parsley and then cooked in parchment becomes an extraordinary entrée, Moroccan-style. Fresh June strawberries poached in orange juice and cardamom pods is an unusually delicious dessert. I show you how to make a surprising hors d'oeuvre with carrots and a pasta sauce with beet tops. I tell you about scalloping, bluefishing, and tuna fishing off Nantucket and then give you some recipes for the catch. I talk to you about the original American dish, succotash, and then make up one that suits today's lifestyle. You need not actually be in Nantucket, for these recipes are made from fresh ingredients available across the country.

My Nantucket table sits under an ancient cedar tree near "Airdrie." The table is laden with food made with picked-when-mature vegetables and freshly caught fish, accompanied by good things to drink. Use this book, smell the rugosa roses, feel the salt spray, sense the Island history, and think about the brave souls who fearlessly forged a life that would inspire future generations. Then you can go to the nearest farm stand, buy some eggplant, tomatoes, corn, and basil, and go home and cook a fast, fresh, and tasty meal to share with family and friends on your own Nantucket table.

A

CHAPTER ONE

PPETIZERS

JAMES BEARD ON NANTUCKET

In 1953 James Beard took a job as manager/head cook at a hamburger joint called Lucky Pierre on Steamboat Wharf in Nantucket. "Oh, what a hamburger joint," recalls Gwen Gaillard, owner of the late, lamented Opera House restaurant. Gwen tells me that along with serving the best burgers—made with choice beef and seasoned brilliantly, sometimes with garlic, sometimes with rosemary (remember, we're talking about the early 1950s)—Beard offered a selection of soups such as pot-au-feu, delicious salads, mussels that he picked off the jetties much to the horror of the locals, and fancy lobster concoctions sitting on little beds of rice. In order to make these more complicated dishes—his gravel-floored, tent-roofed shack with nail-keg stools had only two burners—Beard commandeered Gwen's Opera House kitchen. He would arrive like a clap of thunder, throw everyone out, and turn off the stockpots. Even so, Gwen says he was fun to cook with, and he used her kitchen for everything from brushing his teeth to making a sauce—and chocolate roulades, which he prepared not only for himself, but also for Gwen to offer on the Opera House's dessert menu.

CHICKEN-ALMOND ROUNDS

Makes 4 dozen one-bite sandwiches

Before coming to Nantucket in 1953, the pioneering and entre-preneurial James Beard had a business in New York City called Hors d'Oeuvre, Inc., opened in January 1939. The shop offered New Yorkers who were entertaining—giddy with the end of pro-hibition—a great variety of cooked cocktail-party food. One of the most requested items on this way-before-its-time take-out menu was an onion sandwich made on brioche bread. This was a snack dear to Beard's heart as it was one made for him as a child by his mother. Two slices of brioche were slathered with mayon-naise, then sliced onions were placed on one slice, and the other was set on top to make a sandwich. Three rounds were cut from the sandwich and were squeezed a bit to let some mayonnaise ooze out, then were rolled in chopped parsley. These little onion rounds gained ingredients as time passed. I learned about the Chicken-Almond Rounds about fifteen years ago, far into their evolution.

They're the most popular hors d'oeuvre that I make. They never cease to delight all who eat them. To James Beard—thank you!

4 large boneless, skinless chicken breasts

¾ cup good-quality commercial mayonnaise, plus more as needed

2 celery ribs, peeled and finely diced

1 small red onion, finely diced

2 tablespoons dried tarragon

1 teaspoon salt

½ teaspoon freshly ground white pepper

24 very thin slices white bread

1½ cups roasted salted almonds, chopped in a food processor to the consistency of fine gravel

1. Place the chicken breasts in a large skillet with water to cover. Over medium-high heat, bring to a boil, with the cover askew. Lower the heat a notch and simmer gently until the chicken is opaque throughout. Remove the chicken from the liquid and let cool.

2. Place the ¾ cup mayonnaise in a bowl, and add the celery, onion, tarragon, salt, and pepper. Stir to mix well. Break the chicken into large pieces. Working in 2 batches, use a food processor to chop the breasts until they resemble oatmeal. Add the ground chicken to the celery mixture. Carefully combine with a rub-ber spatula.

3. Line up 4 bread slices at a time. Spread each slice with some of the chicken mixture, forming a layer ¼ inch thick. Cover each slice with a second slice. Repeat until you have 12 sandwiches. Using a 1½-inch-diameter biscuit cutter, cut out 4 rounds from every sandwich, gently pushing them free from the cutter after every 2 cuts. Keep the pairs of rounds stacked together and cover with damp paper towels until all of the sandwiches are cut.

4. Pour the chopped almonds into a baking dish or onto a dinner plate. Holding a stack of sandwich rounds between thumb and forefinger, spread a film of mayonnaise around the cut edges. Roll the stack through the chopped almonds until the edges are completely coated with the nuts. Re-cover the stacks with the damp paper towels until all are coated.

5. To serve, separate each stack back into 2 sandwiches.

CRUDITÉS: HOW TO CUT AND PREPARE

From June through October, Bartlett's Farm truck stand can be seen on Nantucket's Main Street, its tailgate bins laden with the bounty of the warm-weather harvest. The tender young carrots, assorted cherry tomatoes, and jade-color sugar snap peas beckon your attention and immediate purchase. Then what? Crudités, in or out of fashion according to the culinary critics, have always found a permanent place on my appetizer menus. Bartlett's offering makes preparing and assembling a beautiful crudités display pure pleasure.

Carrots: Find the very new or baby carrots with their tops still intact. Break off the tops, leaving about 3 inches of the green stem to use as a handle. Peel the carrots and tidy up the area where the green meets the orange. Wrap in damp paper towels and refrigerate until ready to serve.

Cherry tomatoes: Farmers are always experimenting with different varieties of a species, and cherry tomatoes lend themselves to these efforts brilliantly. There are many, many sizes, shapes, and colors available—choose red, yellow, and orange, round and pear shaped. Rinse and dry on paper towels. Refrigerate until ready to serve. Mix them together to display.

Green beans: Pinch off the vine end of the bean. I like to leave the slender tail with its little curl, as I find it very appealing when the beans are mixed with all the other vegetables. Blanch the beans in boiling water for 10 seconds *at the most,* just enough to bring up the color. Immediately plunge into ice water

to halt the cooking and preserve the color. Dry on paper towels. Refrigerate until ready to serve.

Radishes: Break away all but a few strong leaves. The leaves serve the radish esthetically and function as a handle. Rinse off any dirt under cold running water. Immerse in water and refrigerate until ready to serve. Pat dry with paper towels before serving.

Scallions: Cut off the little beardlike root. Cut down the green part of the leaves so that about $3\frac{1}{2}$ inches, total, remain. Peel away an outside layer or two of leaves (the dirty ones). Rinse and dry on paper towels. Refrigerate until ready to serve.

Sugar snap peas: Snap one end of the pea and pull down to remove the string along the side. Repeat, snapping off the other end and pulling it down the opposite side. To blanch or not to blanch? The peas are delicious raw. If you decide to blanch, immerse in boiling water for no more than 2 seconds. Plunge immediately into ice water. Dry on paper towels. Refrigerate until ready to serve.

Wax beans: Same procedure as green beans.

Zucchini: Choose a mix of green and gold zucchini. Scrub each squash thoroughly. Zucchini grow along the ground and tend to hold a lot of grit. Slice on the diagonal into $\frac{1}{8}$-inch-thick ovals.

Crudités are much more than raw vegetables when accompanied by these sparkling dips. With each carrot dipped into Hummus with Fresh Thyme, with each zucchini oval sunk into Red Pepper–Walnut Dip, a wonderful new taste sensation has been created.

HUMMUS WITH FRESH THYME

Makes a bit less than 1 quart

> 1 can (19 ounces) chickpeas, drained
>
> $\frac{1}{4}$ cup tahini
>
> Grated zest and juice of 1 lemon
>
> 1 clove garlic, sliced
>
> 1 teaspoon ground cumin
>
> 1 tablespoon fresh thyme leaves
>
> 1 teaspoon salt
>
> $\frac{1}{4}$ to $\frac{1}{2}$ cup warm water
>
> Extra-virgin olive oil and sesame seeds for garnish

1. Combine all the ingredients, except the water and garnish, in a food processor. Process for 30 seconds. With the machine still running, slowly add $\frac{1}{4}$ cup of the warm water until the mixture is smooth. You may then continue to run the processor until the hummus is pale beige and the consistency is like sour cream. Add the remaining $\frac{1}{4}$ cup of water if necessary to achieve the desired consistency. Taste and adjust the seasonings. I like hummus to be very smooth and very lemony.

2. Serve the hummus in a shallow bowl. Drizzle with olive oil and sprinkle with sesame seeds.

RED PEPPER–WALNUT DIP

Makes approximately 2 cups

> 1 large egg
>
> 1$\frac{1}{2}$ teaspoons salt
>
> 1 teaspoon sherry vinegar
>
> $\frac{1}{4}$ teaspoon ground cayenne pepper
>
> 1 tablespoon tomato paste
>
> 1 red bell pepper, cut into pieces
>
> $\frac{1}{2}$ cup walnut pieces
>
> About 1$\frac{1}{2}$ cups corn oil

1. Combine the egg, salt, and vinegar in a food processor and process until the egg is frothy. Stop the machine and add the cayenne, tomato paste, half of the red bell pepper, and half of the walnut pieces. Start the machine again and slowly dribble in the corn oil, stopping when a firm mayonnaise forms. (You probably won't need the full amount of oil.) Add the remaining red bell pepper and walnuts and process for a few seconds so that the peppers and walnuts break up into smaller pieces. If you like, save a few pieces of peppers and walnuts from the second addition to use as a garnish when serving the dip.

2. Serve in an attractive bowl garnished with red bell pepper and walnut pieces.

CARROT CROSTINI

Makes 10 dozen crostini

Carrots are one of those "I love them raw, hate them cooked" vegetables. Haters of cooked carrots, as well as full-stop carrot haters, will change their opinion when they try these carrot crostini. This appetizer, at the same time garlicky, sweet, salty, and creamy, comes to my cook's catalogue by way of Italy's Tuscan coast, where vegetables are really the star attraction in all the meal courses. In Nantucket, bright bunches of carrots show up at Bartlett's and Moors End produce stands in June and stay there right through September. Make this carrot topping a day or two before you intend to serve the crostini if you like. Just don't let the summer pass without delighting yourself with this new way to taste carrots.

For the carrot topping

2 cloves garlic, finely minced

$1/2$ cup unsalted butter

10 carrots, peeled and finely grated

$3/4$ cup heavy cream

1 teaspoon salt

1 teaspoon freshly ground white paper

$1/2$ cup finely chopped fresh flat-leaf parsley

For the crostini

3 dense baguettes, each 12 inches long

1 cup corn oil

Kosher salt (see Note)

1. Make the carrot topping. In a skillet over medium heat, sauté the garlic in the butter until golden. Add the carrots and the cream. Reduce the heat and simmer until the carrots are just tender. Remove from the heat and add the salt, pepper, and all but 1 rounded tablespoon of the parsley. Let cool. The mixture will thicken as it cools.

2. Make the crostini: Preheat an oven to 350°F. Cut the baguettes into $1/4$-inch slices. Brush the entire surface of a baking sheet or a jelly roll pan with a bit of the corn oil. Place the bread slices on the sheet or pan. Brush each slice with a bit of corn oil and sprinkle with kosher salt.

3. Bake until the slices are golden, about 10 minutes. Remember that they will continue to cook for a few minutes more after they've been removed from the oven. Repeat until all the slices have been toasted.

4. Mound the cooled carrot mixture on the crostini. Garnish with a sprinkle of chopped parsley.

Note: I always use kosher salt as the shape of the crystals allows it to adhere to food better than normal salt.

RADISH AND ARUGULA SANDWICHES

Makes 4 dozen two-bite sandwiches

Vegetable sandwiches conjure afternoon tea served under a leafy tree, resplendent on a white lace–covered table. They also remind me of children's stories where rabbits live in harmony, for the most part, with humans.

I like to serve these sandwiches with whole radishes, prepared as for crudités, a bowl of unsalted butter, and a dish—or scallop shell—of kosher salt. I show my guests how to dip the radishes in the butter, then in the salt for a yummy radish encore.

24 very thin slices white bread
2 cups sliced radishes
36 to 48 arugula leaves, rinsed and dried
$\frac{1}{2}$ cup unsalted butter, at room temperature
$\frac{1}{2}$ cup good-quality commercial mayonnaise
Salt and freshly ground white pepper

1. Line up the bread in pairs, 4 pairs at a time. "Mask" each slice with a thin film of butter (masking the bread not only adds flavor to the sandwich, but also protects it from becoming soggy). Then spread each slice with a thin layer of mayonnaise.

2. Cover one side of each pair with sliced radishes and the other with 3 or 4 arugula leaves. Sprinkle the radish side with salt and pepper and place $\frac{1}{2}$ teaspoon of mayonnaise in the middle of the slice. Cover with the arugula side, pressing gently but firmly. Trim away the crusts and cut on the diagonal to make 4 triangular 2-bite sandwiches.

3. Serve immediately, or refrigerate, covered with damp paper towels, until ready to serve.

UNDERGROUND VEGETABLES

Nantucket's loamy soil offers a hospitable ambiance for the cultivation of root vegetables. The near absence of clay allows the formation of perfectly straight carrots, globelike radishes, and potatoes that belong in a museum. All things being equal— an uninterrupted growing season, no hurricane-sheared tops, the successful thwarting of underground vermin, and a temperate climate from planting to harvest— the farmer can boast bumper crops of everything that has been seeded.

SCHIACCIATA WITH POTATOES AND ROSEMARY

Makes 4 schiacciate

Schiacciata is the flattest of the Italian flatbreads—flatter than pizza and flatter than focaccia. Schiacciata literally means "squashed." Like the painter's blank canvas, the schiacciata begs to be covered. Potatoes and rosemary are a classic combination. The crisp, waxy flesh of the new potato is perfect for this high-heat, flash-baked bread. Be sure to choose red-skinned new potatoes for purely esthetic reasons.

The little strips of cut-up schiacciata are truly tasty with drinks—but also consider serving them with a salad and call the combination dinner.

For the dough

2¼ teaspoons active dry yeast (one ¼-ounce package)

½ teaspoon sugar

1 cup warm water, about 90°F

3 cups all-purpose flour

2 teaspoons salt

⅓ cup extra-virgin olive oil

For the topping

2 red onions, thinly sliced

4 tablespoons extra-virgin olive oil

6 tablespoons fresh rosemary leaves

2 teaspoons salt

1 teaspoon freshly ground black pepper

1 pound new red potatoes, thinly sliced with a vegetable peeler and steeped in ice water

½ cup grated Parmesan cheese

1. Make the dough: Combine the yeast, sugar, and water (I use a 2-cup Pyrex measuring cup). Let stand until foamy, about 15 minutes. Combine the flour and salt in a large bowl. Add the olive oil to the yeast mixture, then add the yeast mixture to the flour. Mix well. Turn out onto a floured surface. Knead until soft and elastic, 3 to 4 minutes.

2. Swish a few tablespoons of olive oil in a large bowl and place the dough in it. Turn the dough so it's thoroughly covered in oil. Cover and place in a warm draft-free environment to rise. It should double in size in 45 minutes to 1 hour. Punch down. Cut into 4 pieces and return to the bowl. Re-cover.

3. Prepare the topping: In a bowl, mix the sliced onions with 2 tablespoons of the olive oil, the rosemary leaves, and the salt and pepper. Preheat an oven to 450°F.

4. Have ready 2 baking sheets or jelly roll pans. Stretch each piece of dough into a log that measures about 3 inches by 12 inches. Pat down in place on the sheets or pans. Place the onion mixture over the dough. Drain the sliced potatoes and distribute over the onions. Drizzle the remaining 2 tablespoons olive oil over the potatoes. Sprinkle the cheese over each schiacciata. Bake until the crust is golden, 15 minutes.

5. Serve hot from the oven or at room temperature. Cut into 1- to 2-inch pieces to serve.

NEW POTATO FRITTATA

Serves 6 to 8

For sheer gustatory pleasure, the new potato, which begins to appear at Nantucket farm stands somewhere around mid-July, is second only to the first ripe-from-the-vine tomato. Filled with the memory of a potato tortilla that I ate for the first time at a tapas bar in Barcelona—then saw and sampled at every stop in my travels through Spain—I tested and tested recipes with new potatoes, especially those with golden and buttery flesh like Yukon Golds and German butterballs, until I settled on this recipe. It perfectly captures a wonderful food memory and transports it to the present.

½ pound new potatoes

1 yellow onion, thinly sliced

2 rosemary sprigs, each 3 inches long

2 tablespoons pure olive oil

4 large eggs

½ cup water

Salt and freshly ground black pepper

¼ cup grated Parmesan cheese

1. Place the potatoes in a saucepan with water to cover over medium-high heat. Bring to a boil, lower the heat a notch and simmer until the tip of a knife or skewer easily pierces the potatoes. Plunge them into ice water to halt the cooking. Drain and reserve.

2. Sauté the onion and rosemary in the olive oil over medium heat using a 10½-inch cast-iron skillet. When the onions are transparent and starting to caramelize, remove from the heat. Remove the rosemary sprigs from the oil (any leaves that have fallen off can remain).

3. Add the parboiled potatoes to the skillet. Roughly mash the potatoes with a fork. Return to medium heat and sauté for 4 to 5 minutes.

4. Meanwhile, in a bowl, beat the eggs, water, and salt and pepper to taste until the eggs are pale and frothy. Fold in the Parmesan. Pour the egg mixture into the skillet. With a fork, begin to pull back the potatoes to allow the eggs to be fully incorporated. Repeat this process until the eggs appear completely set. Lower the heat a notch, cover, and cook for 7 to 8 minutes, or until the frittata is golden and puffy (it will settle almost as soon as it's removed from the heat). Remove from heat and uncover.

5. Let cool before serving. The frittata should lift out of the skillet with ease. Cut into 1½-inch-wide strips and then into small squares for hors d'oeuvres, or cut into narrow wedges for a buffet.

GRILLED CURRIED TUNA EN BROCHETTE WITH MANGO MAYONNAISE

Serves 10 to 12

Yankee sea captains enriched the larder of their New England pantries with the exotic spices that they brought home with them from their worldwide trading voyages. More than one Nantucket spice shelf included a container of precious curry powder. Even though tuna is now regularly fished off the Nantucket coast, it did not join the Island cook's catalogue until sometime in the 1920s.

Curry and fresh tuna make a delicate marriage, one to be attended to carefully. Too much citrus in the marinade will leech the natural juices from the fish, and overgrilling will dry it out. Follow these directions and you will have the most meltingly moist and delectable tidbit of tuna that you've ever consumed.

For the fish

2 pounds tuna fillet, cut into 1½-inch cubes

Grated zest and juice of 2 limes

2 tablespoons good-quality curry powder

1 large clove garlic, mashed through a press

2 tablespoons fresh thyme leaves or 1 tablespoon dried thyme

1 teaspoon red pepper flakes

¾ cup corn oil

1 tablespoon kosher salt

For the mango mayonnaise

1 ripe mango, peeled, pitted, and cut in small chunks

1 small yellow onion, finely diced

Grated zest and juice of 1 lime

1 teaspoon salt

1 large egg

About 1½ cups corn oil

1. Prepare the fish: Combine the tuna, lime zest and juice, curry powder, garlic, thyme, red pepper flakes, and corn oil in a nonreactive bowl. Cover and let stand for at least 1 hour or for up to 2 hours.

2. Make the mayonnaise: Combine the mango, onion, lime zest and juice, and salt in a bowl and let stand for 1 hour. Place the egg in a food processor and process until frothy and pale yellow. With the motor running, very slowly add enough corn oil to form a thick mayonnaise. Transfer to a bowl and fold the mango-onion mixture into the mayonnaise. Cover and refrigerate until ready to serve. (The mayonnaise will keep for up to 5 days.)

3. Start a fire in a grill 15 minutes before you are ready to cook the tuna. Add the salt to the tuna mixture. (Do not add until you are ready to grill the tuna or it will draw too much moisture from the fish.) Immediately thread the tuna cubes onto 8-inch wooden skewers or decorative metal ones, placing one cube on each skewer.

4. Arrange the loaded skewers on the outside edge of the grill (to prevent the skewers and your fingers from burning). Turn the skewers as necessary, until nicely colored on all sides, about 1 minute on each of 4 sides.

5. Serve with the mango mayonnaise. The bowl of mango mayonnaise looks very nice sitting on the same platter as the tuna brochettes.

Notes: A quick and easy mango mayonnaise can be prepared in minutes by combining 1½ cups good-quality commercial mayonnaise with ½ cup coarsely chopped Major Grey's chutney. Stir well.

It's a good idea to make a "skewer return." Cut a lemon or a lime in half crosswise, then remove a tiny slice from the end so that the half stands up on a platter, ready to receive the emptied skewers.

THE NANTUCKET SEAFEST

The Nantucket Seafest was created in 1979 to promote the Island fisheries. To boost the industry, the consuming public was asked to try nontraditional seafood along with the old New England standbys. To that end, food concessions were operated by Island organizations (the Angler's Club, for example), restaurants, and individuals who participated in food demonstrations and recipe contests, all situated appropriately and picturesquely at Steamboat Wharf. Visitors were able to sample food made with seafood that, though plentiful in the surrounding waters, was underutilized: mussels, monkfish, conch, and squid. There were also dishes made with the popular bluefish, striped bass, cod, and scallops.

Unfortunately, the Seafest no longer exists, but its legacy is here to stay. While James Beard had to endure the ridicule of the public when he offered *moules marinières* on his Lucky Pierre menu, mussels marinara now shows up on any number of local restaurant menus. Squid, once quick-frozen and shipped directly to Japan, now becomes fried calamari on local menus. It's as requested as fried onion rings.

SMOKED BLUEFISH PÂTÉ

Makes 4 cups pâté

Smoked bluefish pâté says "Nantucket" more than any other recipe in this chapter. It is the hors d'oeuvre of choice as soon as cocktails are poured on every deck and in every parlor from 'Sconset to Madaket, from Surfside to Monomoy. Whether you go down to Glidden's Island Seafoods and purchase already-made pâté or, in a matter of minutes, prepare the following recipe yourself, you will enjoy this smoky, bright spread on crunchy crostini (see Carrot Crostini, page 29), on crackers, or as a filling for cherry tomatoes. Garnish with dill sprigs, capers, or grated lemon zest.

1 pound smoked bluefish
2 tablespoons coarsely chopped red onion
$\frac{1}{2}$ cup unsalted butter, at room temperature
1 package (8 ounces) cream cheese, at room temperature
2 teaspoons anchovy paste
Grated zest and juice of 1 lemon

1. Remove the skin and any dark meat from the fish. Break into 2- or 3-inch pieces. Pulse in a food processor for a few seconds, 3 or 4 times, until the fish resembles gravel. Add the onion and pulse for a few seconds. Cut the butter and cream cheese into pieces. Add to the fish and process for 45 seconds. Add the anchovy paste and the lemon zest and juice. Process until the mixture resembles cream cheese.

2. Remove the pâté from the processor and chill before serving. The pâté will stay fresh for 10 days to 2 weeks, refrigerated.

BUTTERMILK-DILL BISCUITS WITH SMOKED SALMON, CUCUMBER, AND SCALLION CREAM CHEESE

Makes twelve 2½-inch or twenty-four to thirty 1½-inch biscuits and 2 cups cream cheese

Fran Jacobs has saved my professional life on more than one occasion. Fran's business is called F. J. Pastries. She and her lively crew supply the caterers and restaurateurs of New York with all those painstakingly fussy mini tart shells, barquettes, vol-au-vents, petits fours, and fancy cookies that would take hours of our kitchen time not to mention all our excess patience.

Fran has kindly shared with me one of her simpler recipes. These light biscuits are as old-fashioned as a Nantucket summer. If you choose to cut the filled biscuits into 2½-inch rounds, they'd be perfect for a beach brunch. If instead you use a 1½-inch biscuit cutter, the tiny biscuits with salmon-cucumber filling seductively slipping out the middle will be the hit of your next cocktail party.

For the biscuits

2 cups all-purpose flour

2 teaspoons baking powder

½ teaspoon baking soda

½ cup plus 2 tablespoons unsalted butter

⅔ cup buttermilk plus ¼ cup buttermilk for glaze

2 tablespoons finely chopped fresh dill plus a few sprigs for garnish

For the cream cheese

1 package (8 ounces) cream cheese, at room temperature

¼ pound diced smoked salmon

½ cup finely diced, peeled, seeded cucumbers

⅓ cup finely chopped scallions

1 teaspoon freshly ground white pepper

1 teaspoon grated lemon zest

1. Make the biscuits: Preheat an oven to 450°F. Sift the dry ingredients into a bowl. Cut in the butter until the mixture resembles cornmeal. Add the ⅔ cup buttermilk and the chopped dill, and stir until the dough forms a ball.

2. Roll out on a thoroughly floured surface to ¼ inch thick. Cut into the biscuit size desired. Place on a baking sheet. Paint the top and sides of each biscuit with buttermilk. Snip pieces of dill from the sprigs and place in the center of each biscuit. Bake until the biscuits are pale gold, 10 to 12 minutes. Let cool completely.

3. Make the filling: Place the cream cheese in a bowl. Fold in the smoked salmon, cucumbers, scallions, pepper, and lemon zest, one by one, fully combining with a rubber spatula. The mixture can be used immediately or stored in the refrigerator for up to 1 week.

4. Split the biscuits with a sharp knife and fill with the cream cheese just before serving.

C

CHAPTER TWO

FIRST
COURSES

EGG-LEMON SOUP WITH CHARD RIBBONS

Serves 4 to 6

Chard is one of those miraculous crops that lasts the entire summer: you just keep picking the outer leaves from the plants. My sister, Laura, grows a variety of rhubarb chard and bietola, an Italian chard—the types I used to test this recipe. I've also made this soup with farm-stand or supermarket Swiss chard with equal results. If you do come across rhubarb chard, try it because it turns the Egg-Lemon Soup, a variation of the classic Greek soup, avgolemono, a gorgeous tangerine color.

$\frac{1}{2}$ **cup converted rice**

4 cups chicken broth or vegetable broth (page 44)

2 large eggs

Juice of 1 lemon

$\frac{1}{4}$ **cup grated Parmesan cheese**

$\frac{3}{4}$ **pound chard**

Salt and freshly ground white pepper to taste

1. Put the rice and broth in a large saucepan over medium heat. Cook the rice until practically over-done, 15 to 20 minutes. Meanwhile, in a bowl, beat the eggs with the lemon juice and Parmesan until pale. Slowly add about one-fourth of the broth to the egg mixture, stirring constantly. This will stabilize the egg mixture so that it won't curdle when you pour it into the rice and broth. Keep it off the heat until then.

2. Break the rib off each chard leaf just where the leaf ends. Pile 3 or 4 leaves on top of each other, then roll tightly lengthwise. Slice this chard "cigar" into $\frac{1}{4}$-inch rounds. When the rounds loosen, they will be perfect ribbons.

3. Repeat until all the chard is cut into ribbons. Combine the egg mixture with the rice and broth. Add the chard ribbons to the soup and cook, covered, over low heat, until the chard is wilted, 10 to 15 minutes.

4. Taste for salt—the Parmesan is salty—and adjust the seasonings. Serve with freshly ground white pepper.

CURRIED CREAM OF FRESH PEA SOUP

Makes about 4 cups broth; serves 6 to 8

Here's another use for that colonial favorite, curry. It's terrific punctuation for the sweet English peas, and the addition of lime juice sparks it all. I like to serve this soup chilled for optimum flavor, though it works very well hot or at room temperature.

For the vegetgable broth
- 6 cups water
- 1 carrot
- 1 celery rib
- 1 small yellow onion
- 1 leek
- 4 flat-leaf parsley sprigs
- 1 bay leaf

For the soup
- ¼ cup finely chopped yellow onion
- 1 tablespoon unsalted butter
- 2 tablespoons peanut oil
- 1 tablespoon good-quality curry powder
- 2 cups shelled peas (about 1¼ pounds in the shells)
- ⅔ cup heavy cream, plus cream for garnish
- Grated zest and juice of 1 lime, plus 1 lime for garnish
- Fresh mint leaves for garnish

1. Make the broth: Add all ingredients to a large saucepan and boil for 5 minutes. Turn down the heat and simmer, cover askew, for 30 minutes. Let cool. Strain.

2. Make the soup: In a large saucepan over medium heat, sauté the onion with the butter and oil until transparent. Add the curry powder, lower the heat a notch, and cook for 2 to 3 minutes. Add the broth and the peas, and simmer until the peas are very tender, 20 to 25 minutes. Remove from the heat and let cool.

3. Purée the soup in a blender until smooth. Add the cream and lime zest and juice. Return to the heat and simmer, whisking all the time so that the cream and lime juice are thoroughly incorporated.

4. Let cool. Chill before serving. Garnish each bowl of soup with a few drops of heavy cream, a lime slice, and a flotilla of 2 or 3 mint leaves.

Note: I usually double or triple the vegetable broth recipe and freeze what I don't immediately use in quart containers.

ISHMAEL AND QUEEQUEG ON NANTUCKET

"Queequeg," said I, "do you think that we can make a supper for both of us on one clam?"

However, a warm savory steam from the kitchen served to belie the apparently cheerless prospect before us. But when that smoking chowder came in, the mystery was delightfully explained. Oh, sweet friends! hearken to me. It is made of small juicy clams, scarcely bigger than hazelnuts, mixed with pounded ship biscuit, and salted pork cut up into little flakes; the whole enriched with butter, and plentifully seasoned with salt and pepper.

Herman Melville
Moby Dick

It was late in the evening when Ishmael and Queequeg arrived in Nantucket to pick up the whaling ship *Pequod*. Peter Coffin, their innkeeper in New Bedford, had directed them to his cousin Hosea Hussey's inn. After some confusion, they found "The Trying-Pots," and Mrs. Hussey immediately sat them down for supper. She gave them a simple choice of "Clam or Cod?" A perplexed Ishmael tried to find out to what she was referring. She just repeated, "Clam or Cod?" "A clam for supper, a cold clam; is that what you mean Mrs. Hussey?" She heard only "clam" and hurried back to the kitchen. It was then that Ishmael asked Queequeg the above question. By the way, after a bowl of the divine clam chowder, they had a bowl of cod chowder as well.

Nantucket Clam Chowder After Mrs. Hosea Hussey

Serves 8

In New England all hard-shell clams are called by the Pequot Indian name, quahog. Quahogs can be littlenecks, cherrystones, or the fully mature "chowder clam" (used for chowder and stuffings because they're deemed too tough for anything else). If fully mature clams aren't readily available where you live, you can honestly say that you've used quahogs to make this authentic clam chowder even if you've used littlenecks or cherrystones. In honor of Herman Melville's Mrs. Hussey, I've used Vermont common crackers, which must be very similar to ship biscuits, to thicken the chowder. Have a supply of extra crackers to serve alongside the chowder.

1/4 pound salt pork or slab bacon, finely diced

1 quart quahogs, packed in 1 cup liquid

2 cups water

1 large yellow onion, finely diced

1/2 cup pounded common crackers (see Note)

2 1/2 cups diced new potatoes

4 cups milk or half-and-half

8 teaspoons unsalted butter

Salt and freshly ground black pepper

1. In a large, heavy-bottomed saucepan or a stockpot over medium-high heat, sauté the pork or bacon until as much fat as possible is rendered and all that remains solid are the cracklings. Remove the cracklings and reserve. Remove all but 2 tablespoons of the fat.

2. Take the quahogs out of their liquid and reserve the liquid. Rinse them in the 2 cups water. Strain the water and reserve. Finely mince the quahogs.

3. Sauté the onion and quahogs together in the pork fat for about 5 minutes. Combine the pounded biscuit with the clam sauté. Add the quahog liquid and the reserved rinse water. Add the potatoes and cook until tender, 10 to 15 minutes. Add the cracklings. In a saucepan, heat the milk or half-and-half; do not boil. Add to the chowder.

4. Serve hot with a teaspoon of unsalted butter in each bowl and salt and freshly ground pepper to taste.

Notes: To break up the crackers, wrap them in a kitchen towel and pound with a wooden or rubber mallet.

To thicken the chowder without using wheat, prepare 1 cup potato purée and add to the chowder instead of the biscuits. Use 2 cups, rather than 2 1/2 cups, diced new potatoes.

COLD BORSCHT WITH ALL THE TRIMMINGS

Serves 6

This borscht tastes like the earth and looks like a Nantucket sunset—and it's the food of my heritage. My Russian grandparents brought this simple soup to the menu of my youth. It was always served cold, in a glass with a dollop of sour cream on top, accompanied on the side by boiled potatoes and eggs. We ate the shredded beets, potatoes, and eggs with spoon and fork until all that remained was the creamy, shocking-pink beet broth. This was imbibed as if it were the best-ever soda fountain concoction.

Beets, like all root vegetables, do extremely well on Nantucket because of the sandy soil and benign climate.

To borscht made with Nantucket beets I add a few extra garnishes: grated lemon zest, chopped fresh dill, and for special occasions, caviar.

For the borscht

1½ pounds beets, shredded

1 small red onion, grated

4 cups chicken broth or vegetable broth (page 44)

Juice of 1 lemon

Salt and freshly ground pepper

For serving

6 rounded tablespoons sour cream

6 teaspoons chopped fresh chives

3 teaspoons finely chopped fresh dill

Grated zest of 1 lemon

6 boiled small, red-skinned new potatoes

3 hard-cooked eggs, sliced in half

1. Make the borscht: In a large nonreactive saucepan over medium heat, cook the beets and onion in the broth until the beets are soft but not mushy, about 45 minutes.

2. Remove from the heat and add the lemon juice and salt and pepper to taste. Chill before serving.

3. To serve, fill iced-tea goblets or glasses with equal amounts of beets and broth. Top each serving with I tablespoon sour cream, I teaspoon chives, ½ teaspoon dill, and a sprinkle of lemon zest. Place each goblet or glass on a salad plate. Place a boiled potato and a hard-cooked egg half on either side of the goblet or glass. Accompany with an iced-tea spoon and fork.

WEST CREEK CAFE ROASTED CORN SOUP

Serves 6

When I asked Pat Tyler, owner of Nantucket's charming West Creek Cafe, if she would share her recipe for the restaurant's excellent roasted corn soup, she referred me to her talented young chef, Dan Ferrare. Dan agreed to give me the recipe, but wondered if I still would want the recipe when I realized that it used so few ingredients. Would I want it? This is exactly the kind of recipe I favor. When you have fresh ingredients to work with, you don't need much else—in this case, summertime's glorious crop, corn. Delicate and distinct, corn shouldn't be put to battle with too many other flavors.

Dan's roasted corn soup honors the food that the Aztecs believed was the food of the gods.

8 ears of corn

4 tablespoons pure olive oil

Salt and freshly ground white pepper

1½ fresh jalapeño peppers, minced

1 yellow onion, coarsely chopped

1 clove garlic, minced

4 cups chicken broth or vegetable broth (page 44)

2 cups heavy cream

3 corn tortillas for garnish

Corn oil for sautéing

1. Preheat an oven to 425°F. Peel each ear of corn down to a single layer of the husk, and cut off the top, brown parts of the silk. Coat the corn using 2 tablespoons olive oil for all 8 ears. Season lightly with salt and white pepper. Place on a baking sheet and roast for 20 minutes, turning once halfway through. Cool to the touch, remove the husks and silk, and scrape the kernels from the cob.

2. Sauté the onion, garlic, and jalapeños in the remaining 2 tablespoons oil in a heavy-bottomed stockpot over medium heat. Add the corn kernels and fully combine. Pour in the broth, lower the heat a notch, and simmer for 20 minutes. Add the cream and simmer for 15 minutes more. Remove from the heat and let cool for about 15 minutes.

3. Purée the soup in a blender until smooth. You may want to strain the soup as well, to eliminate what remains of the skin from the kernels. Taste and adjust the seasonings.

4. Slice the corn tortillas into ⅛-inch-wide strips. Sauté the strips in a small skillet in about 1 inch of corn oil over a medium heat. When the strips start to "ripple," remove with a slotted spoon and drain on paper towels.

5. Serve the soup hot with a garnish of tortilla strips.

Note: I like to add another garnish. Roast a red bell pepper over a gas flame, turning until completely charred. Put it in a bowl, seal with plastic wrap, and keep covered for at least 30 minutes. Peel it and remove the seeds. Purée in a blender. Drop polka dots of red bell pepper purée into each soup serving.

GINGERED BROCCOLI SOUP

Serves 6

When I started my catering business, I devoted part of my store-front kitchen to preparing foods for takeout. One of the most requested items on the menu was this broccoli soup. Its appeal was clearly the interesting combination of ingredients.

Luckily, both of Nantucket's commercial produce farms plant and harvest broccoli twice a year. So, on a chilly spring evening a bowl of this soup, redolent of ginger, will warm you from your nose to your toes. It will do the same in late September when you begin to feel the nippy autumn air.

Juice of $\frac{1}{2}$ lemon or 1 tablespoon vinegar

1 large bunch or 2 small bunches broccoli

1 yellow onion, diced

1 tablespoon unsalted butter

2 tablespoons pure olive oil

1 rounded tablespoon grated fresh ginger, plus 1
   piece fresh ginger, 1 inch by 2 inches, for garnish

$\frac{1}{4}$ teaspoon red pepper flakes

4 cups chicken broth or vegetable broth (page 44)

$\frac{1}{2}$ cup corn oil

1 cup plain, whole milk yogurt

Salt

1 lemon for garnish

1. Fill a bowl with water and add the lemon juice or vinegar. Cut the broccoli into florets and immerse in the acidulated water.

2. In a large saucepan over medium heat, sauté the onion in the butter and olive oil. When the onion is wilted, remove the broccoli from the acidulated water and add to the pan along with the grated ginger and red pepper flakes. Stir to combine and add the broth. Reduce the heat and simmer until the broccoli is soft, about 30 minutes. Let cool.

3. Meanwhile, prepare the garnish: Peel the piece of fresh ginger. Julienne very thinly. In a small skillet over medium-high heat, fry the ginger in the corn oil until golden and crispy, 30 to 45 seconds. Place on paper towels to drain. Thinly slice the lemon.

4. Purée the soup in a blender and return to the pan. Season to taste with salt. Whisk in the yogurt. Heat over low heat to avoid curdling the yogurt.

5. Float 1 or 2 lemon slices on top of each serving of soup. Top the slices with a nest of fried ginger threads.

PASTA E PISELLI

Serves 6 to 8

The simple sweet flavor of early summer peas doesn't need a lot of decoration. The Italians know this—they designed this classic preparation to showcase fresh peas.

Sweet green peas are not unlike corn in that they are best enjoyed if eaten within a couple of hours after they've been picked. If the peas that you are using for this recipe are a day or two old, you might add a pinch of sugar and a few tablespoons of water to the sauce while it's simmering. Choose shells or another round, cuplike pasta shape that will catch and hold the peas and their sauce.

2 tablespoons unsalted butter

2 tablespoons pure olive oil

$1/2$ cup finely diced yellow onion

$2 1/4$ cups shelled peas (about $1 1/2$ pounds in the shells)

$1/4$ cup dry white vermouth

$1/2$ cup chopped fresh flat-leaf parsley

Salt and freshly ground white pepper

1 pound pasta, preferably shells

Grated Parmesan or Romano cheese for garnish

1. In a large saucepan or a stockpot, boil water for the pasta. In a skillet over medium heat, melt the butter with the olive oil and sauté the onion until soft and translucent, 3 to 4 minutes. Add the peas and vermouth. Plunge the pasta into the boiling water and cook. Reduce the heat and simmer the peas until the pasta is cooked, 12 to 15 minutes.

2. Drain the pasta. Add the parsley and salt and pepper to taste to the peas. Toss the pasta with the peas. Serve with the grated cheese.

Note: This recipe serves up to 8 people, but if you're serving fewer people, make the whole recipe because here's something to do with the leftovers. Mix the pasta with a well-beaten egg and some ricotta. Put into an oiled baking dish, sprinkle the top with grated Parmesan cheese, and bake in a thoroughly preheated 350°F oven for 15 minutes.

REAL PASTA AL PESTO

Serves 6

Pasta al pesto is a seaside food, whether it's made with the strong and fragrant basil growing in the warm Atlantic breezes that fan Nantucket's gardens or the tiny-leafed basil growing along Italy's Ligurian coast ventilated by the winds that blow up from Africa. It's one of the most enjoyable dishes you'll ever eat. Make it with the following ingredients—they work well together, and they're the ingredients of summer.

2 cups fresh basil leaves

$1/4$ cup pine nuts

$1/4$ cup walnut pieces

2 cloves garlic

$3/4$ cup grated Parmesan cheese, plus cheese for garnish

2 teaspoons salt

1 cup pure olive oil

1 pound new potatoes

1 pound green beans, preferably haricots verts

1 pound fettuccine

$1/4$ cup unsalted butter, melted

1. Put the basil, pine nuts, walnut pieces, garlic, Parmesan, and salt into a food processor and purée. With the machine running, slowly drizzle in the olive oil (you may not need the full amount) and process until the mixture resembles mayonnaise. The pesto can be made ahead and refrigerated for up to 4 days or frozen for 6 to 8 months; be sure to seal the top of the pesto with a thin film of olive oil before covering.

2. Put the potatoes in a saucepan over medium-high heat with water to cover. Bring to a boil, lower the heat a notch, and cook until the tip of a knife or skewer easily pierces the potatoes. Remove from the heat. Fill the same saucepan with water and bring to a boil. Pinch the vine ends from the green beans. Blanch in the boiling water for 30 seconds (10 seconds if using haricots verts). Immediately plunge into ice water to halt the cooking.

3. In a large saucepan or a stockpot, boil water for the pasta. Plunge the pasta into the boiling water and cook. Meanwhile, thinly slice the potatoes. Decoratively arrange the sliced potatoes and the green beans around the sides of a warm serving platter or individual pasta dishes.

4. Drain the pasta. Mix in the melted butter and the pesto. Place on the platter or in the individual dishes. Serve with grated cheese.

STEVE BENDER'S PASTA CON VONGOLE ALLA PORTOGHESE

Serves 6

My friend Steve Bender tells me there are five ingredients that go into classic seafood preparations, Portuguese style: garlic, fresh cilantro, hot red pepper, olive oil, and white wine. He gives a Venetian pasta with clams a classic Portuguese preparation, and the result is stunning. It is meant to be very garlicky and spicy, but you can adjust the garlic and hot pepper as you like. In true Portuguese style, serve accompanied by boiled potatoes or rice.

- 5 cloves garlic, very thinly sliced
- 1/2 cup fresh cilantro leaves
- 1/3 cup extra-virgin olive oil
- 2 teaspoons finely chopped fresh hot red pepper such as Thai or cayenne
- 1 1/2 cups very dry white wine such as Pinot Grigio
- 4 dozen cherrystone clams, shucked, cut in half, and their liquor reserved
- 1 pound fettuccine or linguine
- Grated Parmesan or Pecorino cheese for garnish

1. In a large saucepan or a stockpot, boil water for the pasta. In a skillet, simmer (do not sauté) the garlic and cilantro in the olive oil. When the cilantro is wilted, add the pepper, then the wine, and finally the clam liquor. Continue to simmer; do not allow to boil. Plunge the pasta into the boiling water and cook.

2. Drain the pasta. Add the clams to the simmering liquid. The clams should cook for as long as it takes to shake all excess water from the pasta. Combine the pasta and the clams in a large, warm serving bowl. Serve with grated cheese.

THE PORTUGUESE ON NANTUCKET

In the mid-eighteenth century when Nantucket whalers headed for the rich fishing grounds of the Pacific Ocean, they needed to sail east toward Africa, because of the trade winds and ocean currents, before going west toward Brazil and around the Horn. On their way, the ships stopped at the Azores and the Cape Verde Islands to pick up local sailors for the voyage. These sailors later returned with the ships to Nantucket to stay and brought with them their native cuisine. The influence of this cuisine is evident in the hearty kale soup, *caldo verde,* every Islander's favorite winter meal, which is invariably accompanied by thick slices of equally popular floury Portuguese bread. Thanks to the heritage of the Portuguese, food items such as salt cod and linguiça are staples in the Island markets.

FUSILLI WITH BEET GREENS AND CHERRY TOMATOES

Serves 6

When you're buying beets for borscht or any other dish, never let the farm-stand attendee cut off the tops. If you're using the beets first, wrap the greens in paper towels, put them in a plastic bag, and store in the refrigerator up to two days—until you're ready to make this delicious pasta. Beet greens have a delicate, mineral flavor, and in combination with the tomatoes and lemon, they become almost ambrosial. I favor spiral-shaped pasta for this sauce because I like the way the greens cling to it.

2 pounds cherry tomatoes, stems removed

1/4 cup plus 1 tablespoon pure olive oil

1 tablespoon unsalted butter

1 clove garlic, finely minced

2 cups coarsely chopped beet greens

1 teaspoon grated lemon zest

1 tablespoon lemon juice

Salt and freshly ground white pepper

1 pound fusilli, gemelli, or other spiral-shaped pasta

Grated Parmesan or Romano cheese, for garnish

1. Preheat an oven to 500° F. In a large saucepan or a stockpot, boil water for the pasta. Thinly coat the cherry tomatoes with the I tablespoon olive oil, place on a baking sheet, and roast until they look "collapsed," about 10 minutes. Meanwhile, in a skillet over medium heat, melt the butter with the 1/4 cup olive oil, and briefly sauté the garlic. Just before the garlic starts to brown, add the greens and sauté for 5 minutes. Add the lemon zest and juice.

2. Plunge the pasta into the boiling water and cook. Remove the tomatoes from the oven and add to the greens. Mash the tomatoes with a fork and fully combine with the greens. Add salt and pepper to taste. Turn off the heat and let stand while the pasta cooks.

3. Drain the pasta, but not until completely dry, so that it absorbs the excess water but not the sauce. The sauce should only coat the pasta. Return the pasta to the saucepan or stockpot and combine with the sauce. Serve on warm plates accompanied by the cheese.

PASTA SWEEPINGS WITH SEETHED SESAME CARROTS

Serves 6

There was a particularly abundant carrot harvest in my sister Laura's garden a few years ago. She was put to the task of creating new ways to eat the surplus crop. Her penchant for pasta and easy-to-execute delicious meals led her to create this unusually tasty and very pretty dish. Because Laura used a variety of pasta shapes—those handfuls of pasta left at the bottom of the box— her husband, Jimmy, dubbed the assortment "pasta sweepings."

The recipe uses a technique of cooking vegetables called "seething," which was a traditional turn-of-the-century method for cooking potatoes. The carrots are simultaneously steamed to tenderness and sautéed to full flavor. The water evaporates, leaving the carrots ready for the next step.

1½ pounds carrots, peeled and shredded

¼ cup plus 1 tablespoon pure olive oil

½ cup water

2 rounded tablespoons finely chopped fresh chives

2 rounded tablespoons finely chopped fresh mint

1 Thai hot pepper, finely minced (about ¼
    teaspoon)

½ cup plain, whole milk yogurt

¼ cup sesame seeds

Salt

1 pound assorted pasta of similar size and weight
    such as penne, conchiglie, fusilli, and rotelle

1. In a large saucepan or a stockpot, boil water for the pasta. In a large skillet over medium heat, combine the carrots with the ¼ cup olive oil and the water. When the carrots are wilted, but not soft, remove from the heat. Plunge the pasta into the boiling water and cook.

2. In a small bowl, mix the chives, mint, hot pepper, and yogurt. In a small skillet over medium-high heat, toast the sesame seeds in the I tablespoon olive oil until light brown, about 30 seconds. Add to the yogurt mixture. Combine the yogurt mixture with the carrots. Season to taste with salt. Put the carrot mixture in a saucepan over very low heat while the pasta is cooking.

3. Drain the pasta and combine with the carrot sauce. Serve in warm bowls.

SPAGHETTI WITH FRESH TOMATO SAUCE, WHITE BEANS, AND ROASTED BROCCOLI

Serves 6 to 8

I made this pasta for the first time one evening toward the end of August. In late August in Nantucket, you can really feel the approaching autumn. The sky starts to change color, and as the sun lowers and comes closer to the horizon, the blue goes from robin's egg to sapphire. The evenings are cool enough to start a fire in the fireplace. However, the days are still warm enough to produce plump, juicy tomatoes. Late August is when the first delicate bouquets of broccoli from the second harvest are again present at farm stands. Make this pasta with the ingredients that straddle summer and fall, and you'll be soothed, satisfied, and warmed.

1 large bunch or 2 small bunches broccoli

¼ cup corn oil

1 teaspoon salt, plus salt to taste

2 cloves garlic, finely minced

2 tablespoons unsalted butter

¼ cup pure olive oil

2 pounds plum tomatoes, peeled and coarsely chopped

½ teaspoon red pepper flakes

1 can (16 ounces) white, navy, or cannellini beans, well drained

1 pound spaghetti

Grated Asiago or extra-sharp white cheddar cheese for garnish

1. Preheat an oven to 500°F. Cut the broccoli in florets; you should have about 8 cups. Place the florets on a baking sheet. Working with your hands, evenly coat the florets with the corn oil and 1 teaspoon salt.

Roast for 15 minutes, turning every 5 minutes. The florets should be slightly golden and crispy.

2. In a skillet over medium heat, sauté the garlic in the butter and olive oil. Just as the garlic starts to turn gold, add the tomatoes and red pepper flakes. Lower the heat a notch and simmer for 15 to 20 minutes. In a large saucepan or a stockpot, boil water for the pasta. Add the beans and roasted broccoli to the sauce. Fully combine all the ingredients. Taste for salt and remove from the heat. Plunge the pasta into the boiling water and cook.

3. Drain the pasta. Mix the pasta with the sauce. Place in a warm bowl and serve with grated cheese.

BAY SCALLOPS AND TOMATOES WITH PASTA SHELLS

Serves 4 to 6

During the 1980 Nantucket Seafest, my cooking demonstration was billed as Italian, so I decided to use this recipe to showcase the Island's world-renowned scallops.

2 pounds plum tomatoes, peeled and chopped, or
    1 can (32 ounces) peeled tomatoes

1 yellow onion, finely chopped

$1/4$ teaspoon red pepper flakes

1 pound pasta shells

2 cloves garlic

$1/2$ cup firmly packed fresh flat-leaf parsley

$1^{1}/_{2}$ pounds bay scallops

Salt

3 tablespoons heavy cream

Grated Parmesan cheese for garnish

1. In a large saucepan or a stockpot, boil water for the pasta. Slowly cook the tomatoes in a nonreactive saucepan over medium heat until reduced by one-third, about 20 minutes. Add the onion and red pepper flakes, and continue to cook. Plunge the pasta into the boiling water and cook.

2. Chop the garlic cloves and parsley together until they form a loose paste. Add the scallops to the sauce and cook until opaque, about 2 minutes. Salt to taste.

3. Drain the pasta. Put half of it in a warm serving dish. Pour the sauce over the top. Add the cream and the remaining pasta. Top with the garlic-parsley paste and toss all the ingredients together. Serve in warm bowls with the grated cheese.

BAY SCALLOPING ON NANTUCKET

According to Clint Andrews in his definitive book, *Fishing Around Nantucket*, the market for the eyes, or adductor muscles, of scallops developed in the late nineteenth century. Until that time, bay scallops were used more as bait to catch other fish. Can you imagine? Nantucket's precious crop was regularly shipped to New York City specifically to supply the legendary Delmonico's restaurant.

The beautiful catboats that tacked back and forth in the harbor pulling their dredges must have been a magnificent spectacle. Now, assorted boats with outboard and inboard motors work off Coatue's shores and bring their valuable catch dockside. And, just as their predecessors did, the fishermen take the scallops to a shanty to be shucked, then to a local buyer who sends them off-island to city markets around the country.

CHAPTER THREE

MAIN
COURSES

CODFISH PARK, 'SCONSET

When the village of Siasconset—known locally as 'Sconset—on the Island's northeastern end began to be settled around 1680, fifty-square-foot shacks were built on the thirty-foot-high bank overlooking the Atlantic Ocean for use as whale-watching shelters. The whalers would launch their small boats from the beach directly below the bank. As whaling became a more important industry and fishermen sailed the world in search of the leviathans, these dwellings were used by fishermen who came from "The Town" (Nantucket) to 'Sconset in spring and fall to catch cod. From time to time their wives would join them. These women, dissatisfied with the crude shacks, initiated the construction of "warts," shedlike additions attached to the original shelter, to enlarge the living space. They were built from bits and pieces of lumber, bricks, wrought iron, and mismatched windows brought from "The Town." The newly spacious cottages forever defined the charming 'Sconset style, and part of this collection of buildings, "below bank" overlooking the Atlantic Ocean, became known as Codfish Park.

SUMMERTIME CODFISH CAKES

Makes eight 3-inch cakes; serves 4

To honor the pioneers of early 'Sconset and their catch, we took the photograph of Summertime Codfish Cakes in the yard of Mina Manner's "Svargaloka" (Sanskrit for "land of Paradise"), a direct descendant of an early fisherman's shack.

1 pound cod fillet

1/3 pound new potatoes

1/4 cup finely chopped scallions

1/2 cup very finely diced red bell pepper

2 tablespoons coarsely chopped fresh flat-leaf parsley

1 large egg, beaten

2 teaspoons salt

Several splashes hot pepper sauce such as Tabasco

3/4 cup unseasoned bread crumbs

1 tablespoon unsalted butter

1/2 cup corn oil

Fresh Fruit Chutney (page 129) or Tartar Sauce (page 130)

1. Bring a skillet of water to a boil over medium-high heat. Immerse the cod in the water and cook for 5 minutes. Remove the fish from the liquid and let cool. Place the potatoes in a saucepan over high heat, with water to cover. Bring to a boil, reduce the heat to medium-low, and cook until the tip of a knife or skewer easily pierces the potatoes. Plunge into ice water to halt the cooking, and drain. Flake the fish and finely dice the potatoes.

2. Combine the cod, potatoes, scallions, bell pepper, parsley, egg, salt, and hot sauce in a bowl. Wet your hands before forming each cake. Make 3-inch-diameter by about $1\frac{1}{2}$-inches-thick cakes, pressing each carefully to assure a firm, solid patty. Thoroughly coat the cakes in the bread crumbs.

3. Melt the butter with the corn oil in a skillet over a medium-high heat. Fry the cakes for about 3 minutes on each side. They should be dark gold when cooked. Drain on paper towels.

4. Serve with Fresh Fruit Chutney or Tartar Sauce.

SALMON COOKED IN PARCHMENT WITH CHARMOULA, CHOPPED GREEN OLIVES, AND LEMONS

Serves 8 to 10

Traditional Nantucket Fourth of July festivities demand a dinner of salmon and peas—seasonal fare—directly connected to the local pea harvest and salmon fishery. I'm always happy to see summer's first peas, but salmon that once was seasonal only in the summer is now so successfully farmed that it's always available. This salmon is made in a style that ensures unusually moist fish, using ingredients that tantalize the taste buds. I like parchment preparation because the fish first marinates for eight to twenty-four hours, then is steamed inside the paper bundle without allowing a drop of natural juice to escape. Once you've tried this style, you may never poach salmon again. The charmoula is a classic Moroccan rub for fish. The choice of spices may vary slightly from Casablanca to Marrakech, but the fresh herbs and lemon juice are essential.

$^3/_4$ cup coarsely chopped fresh cilantro

$^3/_4$ cup coarsely chopped fresh flat-leaf parsley

1 rounded tablespoon ground cumin

1 teaspoon ground cayenne pepper

2 cloves garlic, finely minced

Juice of 1 lemon

$^1/_2$ cup extra-virgin olive oil, plus oil for coating

2 teaspoons salt

Parchment paper twice as long as the fish

1 salmon fillet, 2 to 2$^1/_2$ pounds, deboned and skinned

$^3/_4$ cup coarsely chopped green olives

10 to 12 thin lemon slices, pits removed

1. The day before or at least the morning before the fish is to be served, make the charmoula by combining the cilantro, parsley, cumin, cayenne, garlic, lemon juice, $^1/_2$ cup olive oil, and salt in a bowl.

2. Lightly oil the parchment paper. Place the salmon in the middle of the length of paper. Cover with the charmoula, then with the olives. Place the lemon slices decoratively along the fish. Enclose the fish by folding the paper over from the sides, then the top and bottom, which should meet in the middle. The edges should be made into a small double fold. Instead of folding the double fold into small overlapping folds along the top edge, I simply staple the paper closed. Refrigerate the packet on a baking sheet or platter for at least 8 hours or up to 24 hours. Remove about 1 hour before cooking.

3. Preheat an oven to 500°F. Cook the fish for exactly 11 minutes. The parchment paper will turn golden brown. Serve immediately. For dramatic effect, put the parchment bundle on a serving platter, bring it to the table, slash it open in front of your guests, and listen to the oohs and aahs as fragrant steam is liberated just under their noses.

FIERY GRILLED WHOLE BLUEFISH

Serves 6 to 8

Most people dislike bluefish because they find it's too oily or too strong. I'm sure that the fish they sampled was not fresh or was improperly prepared. Yes, bluefish is oily, but I see this as a plus. Cooking it over high heat, as this recipe does, uses the objectionable oil as a moisturizer and seasons the flesh with an abundance of spice and citrus flavors. Furthermore, the presentation will take your breath away. Be sure to use very, very fresh fish, a few hours old if possible, but no more than two days old, and never, ever frozen fish.

If there are any leftovers, flake the remaining fish off the bones and combine with the spicy filling and a good-quality commercial mayonnaise for a scrumptious bluefish salad.

1 whole bluefish, about 8 pounds, scaled and gutted

1 pound plum tomatoes, peeled and diced

1 cup finely chopped yellow onion

3 rounded tablespoons finely minced fresh ginger

3 cloves garlic, finely minced

1 fresh hot pepper such as cayenne, red jalapeño, or Scotch bonnet, finely minced (about 1 rounded teaspoon)

Grated zest and juice of 2 limes

$1/2$ cup firmly packed, coarsely chopped fresh cilantro leaves

$1/4$ cup pure olive oil

1 tablespoon salt

Aluminum foil two and a half times as long as the fish

1. Start a fire in a grill. Place the fish on a cutting board. Starting just below the gills, make deep (all the way to the bone) vertical cuts, $1\frac{1}{2}$ inches apart, until you reach the tail. Repeat on the second side.

2. In a bowl, combine the tomatoes, onion, ginger, garlic, hot pepper, lime zest and juice, cilantro, olive oil, and salt. Generously stuff this mixture into each of the slits. Fold the foil in half and place the fish on it. Turn up the sides of the foil around the fish in order to catch and hold the escaping juices.

3. Place the fish on the hot grill and cook, covered, for 20 minutes. Uncover and cook for 20 minutes more. The skin on the top side should be slightly crispy. Serve piping hot or at room temperature.

BLUEFISHING ON NANTUCKET

Bluefish, which are completely identified with Nantucket, don't have a history like that of the equally renowned scallops. Bluefish have always been a sport fish, rather than a commercial fish.

Sports fishermen who stand silently at sunset and sunrise along the shores of the beach casting into the surf, and those who go out on their boats to fish at every available moment, will talk endlessly about the thrill of the sport. Once hooked, bluefish fight, kicking and biting to their death. When the fish are reeled ashore or on board, their "choppers," as their teeth are called, are still chomping at the wire leaders. Many a fisherman has been seriously bitten by these ferocious fighters. Undeterred, the fishermen return to fish again and again. It's not because they enjoy eating the fish, not nearly so much as catching them. As a result, the fish that aren't given away to family and friends are sold for a few cents a pound to local fish markets and restaurants.

NANTUCKET BAKED BLUEFISH

Serves 4 to 6

This recipe has been passed around Nantucket more than any other one I know. I saw a version of it in Vogue *magazine more than twenty years ago, and I've seen it in self-published local cookbooks and anthologies of Cape Cod and the Islands recipes. It was also written on a slip of paper tucked inside one of my late mother's cookbooks. There's good reason that this recipe is so often repeated—it's delicious! The heavy-duty ingredients that go into the topping probably do the best job of disguising and at the same time complementing that infamous bluefish flavor. Here's a hint: Take a good look at the fillets. If there appears to be a lot of dark meat on the underside of the fish, cut it away. That's the strong-tasting part of the fish.*

3 pounds bluefish fillets
Unsalted butter for greasing baking dish
1 teaspoon salt
1 teaspoon freshly ground black pepper
1½ cups sour cream
½ cup good-quality commercial mayonnaise
3 tablespoons chopped fresh chives
3 tablespoons lemon juice

1. Preheat an oven to 400° F. Wash and pat dry the fillets. Butter a baking dish and place the fillets in it. Rub them with the salt and pepper. In a bowl, combine the sour cream, mayonnaise, chives, and lemon juice. Cover the fish with this mixture.

2. Bake for 20 minutes, or until fish is firm and opaque all the way through. Then set under a broiler for 5 minutes to brown. Serve piping hot.

BUTTERMILK-AND-HERB-SOAKED CHICKEN-FRIED COD

Serves 4 to 6

Nowadays catching cod for Nantucket consumers isn't quite as easy as launching a boat off the beach in 'Sconset. Fishermen leave the ports of Nantucket, New Bedford, and Gloucester for the Georges Bank, out in the Atlantic off the coast of Massachusetts, where at one time there seemed to be an inexhaustible supply of cod. The fish was so completely identified with the state that the prominent peninsula located on its southeast coast was named Cape Cod. A frenzy of cod harvesting by an international fleet almost depleted the supply, and it took a global agreement to finally regulate the fisheries and (for the time being) to save the most popular fish in the world.

Never mind tuna—cod is the real chicken of the sea, lending its thick, mild white flesh to a variety of preparations. I thought, Why not fry it like my favorite southern fried chicken? Guess what? It worked! I like to serve the fish with Roasted Sweet Potatoes, Corn, and Red Peppers (page 121).

1½ pounds cod fillet

1 cup buttermilk

1 rounded teaspoon paprika

½ rounded teaspoon crumbled dried sage

½ rounded teaspoon crumbled dried rosemary

½ rounded teaspoon crumbled dried thyme

½ teaspoon freshly grated nutmeg

½ teaspoon ground allspice

1 cup flour

1 rounded teaspoon kosher salt

Freshly ground black pepper

Corn or other vegetable oil for frying

1. Cut the cod into 2-inch pieces. In a bowl, combine the cod with the buttermilk and herbs and spices. Soak at room temperature for at least 1 hour and not more than 3 hours.

2. In a shallow bowl, mix together the flour and salt and pepper to taste. Fill a medium skillet halfway with oil and heat over medium to high heat until the oil reaches about 350°F on a deep-fat thermometer.

3. Remove the cod from the buttermilk mixture. Coat 3 pieces at a time with flour and fry until golden and crispy, turning once, about 6 minutes total. Drain on paper towels. Serve immediately on a warm platter.

EAST-EAST-EAST GRILLED STRIPED BASS

Serves 6

When I'm not happily residing on the East End of Nantucket, I'm to be found in a bit more harried state in Manhattan's East Village. My New York home is an arm's length from a whole block dedicated to Indian restaurants and around the corner from a group of East Indian grocery stores. The exotic aromas wafting out invite you in, and once inside you are met with a dazzling assortment of spices, herbs both fresh and dried, nuts, dried fruits, dried beans, grains, rice, and so on. My kitchen has jars and other containers filled with these ingredients. Each year, before I leave for Nantucket, I siphon off a little of each to bring with me. They work well with all the fresh food on the Island. The striped bass, with its agreeable flesh, is the perfect foil for my New York–Indian booty. I cook this fish on an outdoor grill. It remains on aluminum foil the entire cooking time, so you could just as easily roast the fish in a 450°F oven.

2 cups plain, whole milk yogurt

Grated zest and juice of 2 limes

1 cup coarsely chopped fresh cilantro leaves

2 tablespoons mustard oil (see Note)

1 teaspoon cumin seeds

2 cloves garlic, mashed through a press

2 teaspoons red pepper flakes

2 tablespoons kosher salt

1 striped bass fillet, about 3 pounds

Aluminum foil two and a half times as long as
    the fish

1. In a bowl, whisk together all the ingredients except the fish and foil. Let stand for 45 minutes to 1 hour to blend the flavors.

2. Start a fire in a grill. Place the fish in a baking dish and cover with the yogurt mixture. Fold the foil in half and place the yogurt-covered fish on it. Quickly make a bundle to avoid losing the yogurt mixture. Fold closed at the top.

3. Cook on the hot grill for about 20 minutes, or until the fish is firm and opaque all the way through, opening the foil bundle about halfway through the cooking. Serve immediately.

Note: In this application, the mustard oil loses its pungency when cooked and becomes rather sweet, though it's still mustardy.

THE STRIPED BASS

Only just recently have Nantucket's bass-fishing enthusiasts been able to return to their much-loved sport. The fish had been the unfortunate victims of excessively polluted water in their Chesapeake Bay spawning ground. Strict government regulations and full cooperation from the state of Maryland have allowed the bass to return in amazing and healthy numbers.

When, on moonlit summer nights, you see the silhouettes of fishermen at Smith's Point, Surfside, or Cisco, poles in hand, patiently waiting for the night-feeding fish to bite, you know by their gear that they're fishing for bass. Bass fishermen need a heavy jig to catch the clever fish, which have the good sense to swim below the voracious bluefish. The piranha-like bluefish gobble up everything in sight, while the refined striped bass carefully choose what they eat, preferring sea robins.

Let's treasure the reappearance of the delectable striped bass by learning well the lesson of the past and respecting the ocean habitat.

MONKFISH IN SAGE SAUCE

Serves 4 to 6

Monkfish has always been caught in American waters by fishermen who are trawling for more popular fish like flounder, cod, and sea scallops. Lacking a market, these monsters of the deep were thrown back into the ocean, discarded as "junkfish." Now referred to as "poor man's lobster," monkfish is appreciated for its exquisite, delicate flavor and firm flesh. This classic preparation, which brilliantly showcases the fine flavor of the fish, comes from the Mediterranean region, where monkfish was never thrown back into the sea. The Italian name, coda di rospo, *literally means "tail of the toad"—acknowledging that only the tail end of this extremely ugly fish with an enormous bony head is used in cuisine. Whole fresh sage leaves or sage sprigs make a nice garnish for the finished dish.*

    2 pounds monkfish, cut into 2-inch steaks
    Juice of 2 lemons
    2 teaspoons freshly ground white pepper
    8 fresh sage leaves
    2 cloves garlic
    2 teaspoons kosher salt
    2 tablespoons unsalted butter
    2 tablespoons pure olive oil
    About 1$\frac{1}{2}$ cups unseasoned bread crumbs

1. Place the steaks in a shallow dish and marinate in the lemon juice and pepper for at least 1 hour, but not longer than 2 hours.

2. Combine the sage leaves, garlic, and kosher salt in a mortar, and use a pestle to grind into a paste. Melt the butter with the olive oil in a heavy skillet over medium heat. Very slowly add the sage paste, stirring constantly. When the paste is well integrated with the oil and butter, take the monkfish steaks from the marinade (reserve the marinade), and coat them with the bread crumbs, pressing firmly to make sure that the crumbs adhere to the fish. Drop the steaks into the skillet. Cook slowly over medium heat, turning the steaks once, until golden, about 4 minutes on each side. Place on a warm platter.

3. Add the marinade to the skillet and stir to incorporate with the remains of the fish. Cook for 7 to 8 minutes over low heat to thicken it slightly into a sauce. Pour over monkfish steaks and serve immediately.

SUMMER SUNSET SEAFOOD STEW

Serves 4 to 6

The culinary traditions of every city or village that sits at the edge of water includes a version of seafood stew. Whether it's called jambalaya, caciucco, chowder, or bouillabaisse, it always includes a variety of the locally caught fish combined with native vegetables. I'm partial to tomato-based stews. I made this stew for the first time one summer at the end of August. I had a rich supply of local ingredients: fat plum tomatoes, tiny new bliss potatoes, corn on the cob, a tub of parsley, and three dozen littleneck clams. I supplemented this supply with some mussels, monkfish, and an orange. Almost blinded by the bright coral sunset coming through my west-facing kitchen window, I created this very red stew, which now shows up every August on my dinner table. The stew can be served in the style of jambalaya with rice; or caciucco, with a thick slice of dense bread in the bottom of the bowl; or chowder, with crackers; or bouillabaisse, with croutons and garlic mayonnaise.

2 cloves garlic, mashed through a press

1/2 teaspoon red pepper flakes

1/4 cup pure olive oil

2 teaspoons fennel seeds

1 orange

2 pounds plum tomatoes, peeled and coarsely chopped

1 cup dry white wine

1 cup water

1 tablespoon fresh thyme leaves

1 pound tiny red new potatoes, left whole, or 1 pound red new potatoes, cut into 1- to 1 1/2-inch pieces

Kernels from 2 ears of corn

3 dozen littleneck clams, scrubbed

6 pounds mussels, scrubbed and beards removed

2 pounds monkfish or any firm, white-fleshed fish, cut into 2-inch pieces

1/2 cup firmly packed, finely chopped fresh flat-leaf parsley

1. In a large nonreactive stockpot over medium heat, sauté the garlic and red pepper flakes in the olive oil for 1 to 2 minutes. Add the fennel seeds, quickly followed by the tomatoes. Lower the heat a notch and simmer the tomato sauce for 10 minutes. Using a vegetable peeler, remove 3 pieces of zest, each 2 inches by 1/2 inch, from the orange, then juice the orange. Add the orange zest and juice, wine, water, and thyme leaves to the pot. Simmer for 5 minutes. Add the potatoes and simmer for 10 minutes. Add the corn kernels.

2. Add the clams, mussels, and monkfish. Cover the pot and cook until the shellfish have opened, 5 to 8 minutes. Stir in the parsley. Discard any unopened shellfish and serve immediately.

Note: You can hold the stew after adding the corn. The fish takes up to 8 minutes to cook and then should be consumed immediately.

Tuna Fishing off Nantucket

I'm told by tuna fisherman par excellence, Peter Kaizer, that the best tuna in the world is caught right here between the Nantucket shoals and Maine. Why is this so? It's the bait—as simple as that. Somewhere in the Caribbean, tuna swim into the Gulf Stream and head north following the bluefish, which they love to eat. The bluefish in turn are following the squid, sand eels, and herring. When the tuna arrive along the northeast coast to stay for a few months, they snack on krill. These tiny shrimplike organisms thrive in these waters because of the dramatic temperature changes. The food chain offers so much to eat that the tuna are very fat by late August in preparation for the return trip to the West Indies in October— that is, if Peter Kaizer doesn't have his way. Determined and disciplined, Peter is the darling of the Japanese buyers of fish for sushi, simply because his tuna is so carefully handled on and then off the hook. His primary catch is bluefin tuna, and we in Nantucket are lucky to be there when he saves a piece of fish from certain sushi and sells it to the local fish market. The fish markets mostly sell yellowfin tuna, which is a tad leaner than bluefin but nothing to ignore.

GRILLED LEMON-MARINATED TUNA WITH CHERRY TOMATO SPLAT

Serves 6

It was with this recipe for cherry tomato splat, served for the first time with grilled salt cod, that I attracted Tom Eckerle's attention. Tom, food photographer extraordinaire, became so intrigued with this particular preparation that we immediately started talking about the possibility of working together on a book. The Nantucket Table is the happy result.

On Nantucket, I make splat with the surfeit of cherry tomatoes that ripen in abundance all summer, then pair it with Island fresh tuna, grilled in this style.

For the tuna

4 fresh rosemary sprigs, each about 4 inches long

3 pounds center-cut tuna, cut into 6 slices about 2 inches thick

½ cup pure olive oil

Grated zest and juice of 1 lemon

For the splat

1 lemon

2 fresh rosemary sprigs, each about 4 inches long

1 clove garlic, sliced paper-thin

2 teaspoons finely minced fresh red hot pepper such as Thai or jalapeño

1 teaspoon salt

¼ cup extra-virgin olive oil

2 pounds cherry tomatoes, stems removed

1. Prepare the tuna: Remove the leaves from the rosemary sprigs. In a shallow bowl, marinate the sliced tuna with the rosemary leaves, olive oil, and lemon zest and juice for about 1 hour.

2. Make the splat: Preheat an oven to 500° F. Peel the zest from the lemon, using a vegetable peeler, and finely julienne. Juice the lemon. Combine the lemon zest and juice, rosemary, garlic, hot pepper, salt, and oil in a heatproof bowl. Place the tomatoes on a baking sheet or jelly-roll pan and roast for 12 minutes. Immediately place the roasted tomatoes into the heatproof bowl. Smash them with a fork (some of the tomatoes will splash and splat) and incorporate with the other ingredients. The intense heat of the roasted tomatoes will cook the other ingredients.

3. Start a fire in a grill. Grill the tuna for 2 minutes on each side. It should be pink, not rare, in the center. Serve immediately with the tomato splat.

BAY SCALLOPS ALLA VENEZIANA

Serves 4

Sometime toward the end of January when the supply of bay scallops started to dwindle and the days out in the harbor grew longer, I would excuse myself from the crew of Gale Winds *and take my hard-earned scallop dollars and go off to spend the spring in Italy. It was in the beautiful Byzantine city of Venice that I learned how to cook scallops in this style—without a doubt another reward for my wintertime labor.*

For the Parmesan toasts

1 loaf dense Mediterranean-style bread, cut into
  $\frac{1}{4}$-inch slices
$\frac{1}{4}$ cup pure olive oil
$\frac{1}{4}$ cup grated Parmesan cheese

For the scallops

2 cloves garlic, finely minced
$\frac{1}{4}$ teaspoon finely minced fresh red hot pepper
  such as Thai, cayenne, or jalapeño
$\frac{1}{2}$ cup extra-virgin olive oil
2 tablespoons fresh lemon juice
$\frac{1}{2}$ cup dry white vermouth
$1\frac{1}{2}$ pounds bay scallops
$\frac{1}{2}$ cup firmly packed, finely chopped fresh flat-leaf
  parsley
Salt

1. Make the Parmesan toasts: Preheat an oven to 350°F. Spread a thin film of olive oil on a baking sheet. Place the bread slices on the prepared sheet. Sprinkle a bit of cheese on each slice. Drizzle the oil over the slices. Bake until pale gold, 10 to 15 minutes.

2. Make the scallops: In a skillet over medium heat, sauté the garlic and hot pepper in the olive oil. Just as the garlic starts to turn gold, add the lemon juice and vermouth. Lower the heat a notch and simmer 2 to 3 minutes. Add the scallops and cook until opaque, 2 to 3 minutes. Be very careful not to overcook, or the scallops will become rubbery in an instant. Stir in the parsley. Taste for salt.

3. Serve from a warm platter or on warm plates with the Parmesan toasts.

MY YEARS AS A SCALLOPER

It was the best job I've ever had, and it was the most physically demanding job I've ever had. For six years I fished for the extraordinary bay scallops that live in Nantucket harbor. Every first of November, opening day for commercial scallopers, my brother-in-law, Jimmy, and I quietly slipped out of the marina on his boat, pretty lap-strake *Gale Winds,* and headed toward the world's most spectacular sunrise. When we reached a place that Jimmy determined to be a good spot for scallops, the motor was slowed to an idle and the first dredge was dropped in the water, then the second one and so on, until all eight dredges were in place. As the motor was accelerated slightly, the boat advanced until the up and down movement of the dredge warps stopped, signaling that they were full. Each dredge was hauled out of the water and dumped on the culling board, a platform that extended across the boat from port to starboard. It was my job to sort through the contents and discard everything but the live adult scallops.

The scallops are opened by hand immediately after they are caught. They wouldn't live for more than twenty-four hours if permitted to stay inside their shells. They're very active even out of the water and insist on clapping about, opening and closing. At about 8 p.m., Jimmy took the gallon buckets filled to the brim with plump, rosy-colored scallops to town to sell, more than fourteen hours after our day had begun.

OUTDOOR COOKING

Beginning at the end of the seventeenth century and continuing through the middle of the nineteenth century, the biggest celebration on Nantucket was Sheep Shearing Day. Every year in mid-June, seven to eight thousand Island sheep were herded to a central location and washed in preparation for shearing day. The most popular location was an area near Miacomet Pond. A tent, The Big Tent, was erected on the field next to the pond to house the festivities that included dancing and gypsy fortune-tellers. Smaller tents accommodated food vendors' booths that offered for sale an enormous variety of food. The most popular items were fish and meat roasted on outdoor grills and brought inside. In 1839, according to the local paper, the *Inquirer,* some of the roasted food for sale included salmon, whole pigs, ham, mutton, veal, and "beef-steak swimming in butter."

While Sheep Shearing Day is no longer a Nantucket holiday, cooking outdoors on the Island continues to be a desirable way to prepare meals. Whether the summer is feted with a clambake, introduced to the New England colonists by the Native Americans, or everyday meals that are barbecued over a charcoal or gas grill, the feeling and taste are still those of a holiday.

LAURA SIMON'S BEST NANTUCKET BARBECUE SAUCE

Makes 3 cups, enough to marinate 5 pounds meat;
serves 6 to 8

In addition to their magnificent gardens and orchard, my sister, Laura, and her husband, Jimmy, keep bees. The honey produced at their Eat Fire Spring Apiary is as rich as the flora of all Nantucket. The bees feast on the flowers of the garden; the fruit tree blossoms; teasel, their favorite snack, planted especially for them by Laura; and cranberry blossoms from the bog a short flight away. This is the honey that goes into this sweet, spicy, and citrusy barbecue sauce. In lieu of Nantucket honey, search out a good-quality pure *honey.*

This is another recipe that you may as well double—it will keep in the refrigerator for the whole summer. It's a great solution for a last-minute special dinner.

³/₄ **cup dark soy sauce**

Grated zest and juice of 3 limes

2 rounded tablespoons grated fresh ginger

1 cup *pure* **honey**

3 teaspoons dark molasses

1 can (6 ounces) tomato paste

2 teaspoons red pepper flakes

3 cloves garlic, mashed through a press

1 chicken, about 3 pounds, cut into pieces

2 pounds country-style pork ribs

1. In a bowl, combine all the ingredients except the chicken and ribs. Place the chicken pieces and ribs in separate bowls and divide the sauce between them. Marinate, refrigerated, for 6 hours or more. Bring to room temperature before grilling.

2. Start a fire in a grill. Remove the chicken and ribs from the sauce and reserve the sauce. Grill each chicken piece and each rib for approximately 6 minutes per side, or until the juices flow clear from the chicken and the ribs when they are pricked. Brush with the excess sauce every 3 minutes. Serve hot or at room temperature.

GRILLED CHICKEN WITH PANZANELLA STUFFING

Serves 4

My friend Tom Pearson is serious about food—he likes to eat and he likes to cook. He's learned to cook by asking questions, reading cookbooks, and watching the occasional televised cooking program. It was one of Jacques Pépin's PBS programs on the technique of deboning a chicken that forever captured Tom's imagination. Ah, the possibilities of that deflated bird just waiting to be filled.

When Tom and his wife, Marian Young, visited me on Nantucket a few summers ago, he kindly deboned a chicken for me to fill with one of my favorite summertime salads made with slurpy, sun-ripened tomatoes—the Italian tomato and bread salad called panzanella. You can ask a butcher to debone a chicken, or you can do it yourself by carefully following the instructions in various cookbooks, including The Joy of Cooking *and Julia Child's* Mastering the Art of French Cooking.

2 cups toasted bread cubes, 1 inch square, using dense Mediterranean bread

1 cup peeled, seeded, and diced tomatoes

1/2 cup chopped fresh basil

1 tablespoon capers

1 yellow onion, thinly sliced

2 tablespoons extra-virgin olive oil

1 teaspoon kosher salt

1 teaspoon freshly ground black pepper

1 whole chicken, about 3 pounds, deboned

3 feet cotton butcher's twine

1. In a bowl, combine the bread, tomatoes, basil, capers, onion, olive oil, salt, and pepper and let stand for 20 minutes before filling the chicken.

2. To fill the chicken, begin with the legs and thighs, then fill the wing area. The remainder goes in the middle of the chicken—the breast area. Make sure to stuff the bird generously; the stuffing will shrink a bit as it cooks. Close the chicken by placing one piece of breast skin over another. Push the chicken gently with the palms of your hands to form a loglike shape.

3. Tie the legs together at the foot joints with the butcher's twine, knotting the twine and leaving a long tail. Bring the twine along the bottom of the chicken back to the other end. Loop the twine over the top of the chicken and begin to secure the bird together following the directions in the recipe for grilled beef fillet recipe (page 94). Place the chicken on a rack set in a roasting pan. Choose an inexpensive aluminum pan whose sole purpose is to be used in the grill. Fill the bottom with water.

4. Prepare a fire in a grill, using one of two methods. For both methods, use pieces of fruitwood that have been soaked in water for 30 minutes.

For a gas grill: Divide the lava rocks in half and push them to the sides of the grill. Leave the grid off. Turn on the grill. When thoroughly heated, put a few pieces of soaked fruitwood on the rocks. Close the lid of the grill. Let smoke for 5 minutes. Place the roasting pan with the chicken in the middle of the lava rock and fruitwood "nest." Cook for approximately 1 hour, turning the chicken every 20 minutes. Check to make sure there's always water in the pan to prevent burning.

For a charcoal grill: Make a nest in the grill that will accommodate the roasting pan. If you are using real charcoal, there's no need for additional wood; if you're using briquettes, place soaked fruitwood on them when they're white-hot, and replace as needed. Make sure the vents of the grill are open. The chicken may need only 45 minutes with this type of grill; turn every 15 minutes.

Each method should produce a burnished, bronzed-skin chicken that is tender and moist.

5. Let the chicken stand for a few minutes before serving. Remove the butcher's twine, slice, and serve.

GRILLED LEMON MEAT LOAF

Serves 6

Inspired by a recipe from Edda Machlin Servi's The Classic Cuisine of the Italian Jews, *I made this grilled meat loaf in Nantucket on one unusually hot July evening for a group of friends. They couldn't believe that meat loaf could be grilled. So they were both impressed and delighted with the meal they were served.*

The classic Italian meat loaf, or polpettone, *is made with, among other ingredients, bread soaked in milk and Parmesan cheese. This mix of meat and dairy won't do in a kosher kitchen, but in the Italian kosher kitchen, the bread is soaked in lemon juice and the cheese is eliminated. To my mind this makes for an even more tasty creation. The lemon juice is a good contrast to the meat, and the resulting flavor is very clean and bright.*

2 cups bread cubes, $^1\!/_2$ inch square, using dense
   Mediterranean bread
Grated zest and juice of 2 lemons
2 pounds ground beef
2 large cloves garlic, finely minced
$^3\!/_4$ cup coarsely chopped fresh flat-leaf parsley
2 large eggs, well beaten
2 teaspoons salt
$^1\!/_4$ teaspoon freshly ground white pepper
$^1\!/_4$ teaspoon freshly ground black pepper

1. In a bowl, soak the bread cubes in the lemon zest and juice for 45 minutes. Add the beef, garlic, parsley, eggs, salt, and white and black pepper. Using your hands, thoroughly and carefully blend all the ingredients. Form the meat mixture into a loaf measuring approximately 8 inches by 4 inches. Wrap tightly in plastic wrap and chill for at least 1 hour before grilling—more if possible as the loaf needs to be very cold in order to slice evenly.

2. Start a fire in a grill. Slice the loaf into $^3\!/_4$-inch slices. Grill for 2 minutes on each side, or until nicely browned. The meat will not be too rare; the lemon juice has already done its share of cooking the meat. Overgrilling will produce a very dry meat. Serve immediately.

GRILLED FILLET OF BEEF WITH SPICY SUMMER SALSA

Serves 10 to 12

As soon as I arrive on the Island in August, I'm thrilled to see that the farm stands have an endless supply of the ingredients needed to make this salsa. This entrée is the one that I make annually for my first dinner party. I've watched friends who swear they never eat red meat salivate at the sight of this grilled fillet. I think it's because the salsa so successfully saturates and flavors the meat that the dominant cooking aroma is not that of grilling meat, but rather that of grilled vegetables. Enjoy this fillet hot off the grill or at room temperature, or as yummy fillet sandwiches the next day.

For the salsa

  2 pounds tomatoes, peeled, seeded, and finely diced

  1 yellow bell pepper, finely diced

  1 green bell pepper, finely diced

  1 red onion, finely diced

  2 cloves garlic, finely minced

  $^3/_4$ cup coarsely chopped fresh flat-leaf parsley or cilantro

  2 teaspoons finely minced fresh red hot pepper such as Thai or cayenne

  $^1/_4$ cup extra-virgin olive oil

  2 tablespoons balsamic vinegar

  1 tablespoon kosher salt

For the beef

  1 fillet of beef, about 3 pounds, cleaned and trimmed

  4 feet cotton butcher's twine

1. Make the salsa: Combine all the ingredients in a bowl.

2. Prepare the beef: Make a 2-inch-deep cut along the center length of the fillet. Fill this opening with the salsa, packing in as much as you can. Put some salsa under the flaps at the thick end of the meat. There will be leftover salsa. Fold about 3 inches of the thin end of the beef underneath itself. Start a fire in a grill.

3. Here's the difficult part—tying the fillet. Tie and knot the butcher's twine around the thick end, leaving the remaining length of twine loose (about $3^1/_2$ feet). Pull the twine along the bottom, or unstuffed side, of the meat, then bring it back over the top at the other, narrower end. Pull the twine about 3 inches over the end and tightly hold it in place with the index finger of the hand that is not doing the wrapping. Continuing to hold the twine with your finger, loop the loose piece around and under the meat, and back up. Thread through the twine at the point where your finger is holding it. Repeat this process of wrapping and securing the butcher's twine around the fillet at 3-inch intervals until you've reached the other end. Tie the end to the first knot. As you work, keep pushing the salsa down into the center cut.

If you find this process too daunting, simply knot the twine around the thick end of the fillet, draw the long end along the bottom of the meat, loop it around the thin end, and pull it along the top to the first knot and secure. Cut the remaining twine into 6-inch pieces and tie the fillet together at equal intervals along the length.

4. Cook on a very hot grill until the interior temperature reaches 120°F on an instant-read thermometer inserted into the thick end, 15 to 20 minutes. Turn frequently so that all sides are seared. Let stand for a few minutes before slicing. Serve with the remaining salsa.

GRILLED EGGPLANT AND ZUCCHINI LASAGNA

Serves 8

Here's what I like to do with the bounty of eggplant and zucchini harvested on Nantucket starting in midsummer. I cook the eggplant and zucchini on the outdoor grill, but you can oven-roast these vegetables just as successfully. I call this dish a lasagna, even although there are no noodles in it—the grilled vegetables serve the same purpose, albeit much more flavorfully, of sandwiching the luscious cheeses and sauces.

Kosher salt, as needed

3 small or 2 medium eggplants, cut lengthwise into
   1/4-inch slices

6 zucchini, cut lengthwise into 1/4-inch slices

Olive oil for coating vegetables

1 pound whole milk ricotta

2 large eggs, well beaten

1 recipe for Pesto (page 56)

1 recipe for Tomato Sauce (page 131)

1 pound fresh whole milk mozzarella, thinly sliced

Whole basil leaves for garnish

1. Salt alternate layers of the eggplant slices, place in a colander, cover the top layer with paper towels, and weight with a heavy object such as a cast-iron skillet. Let drain for 30 minutes. Rinse and pat dry. Brush the eggplant and zucchini slices thoroughly on both sides with olive oil. Preheat an oven to 350°F. Start a fire in a grill.

2. Cook the vegetables on a very hot grill for about 2 minutes on each side, or until slightly golden. Keep the cooked eggplant and zucchini separate. In a bowl, combine the ricotta, eggs, and all but 1 rounded tablespoon pesto.

3. Layer the ingredients in a 2-quart baking dish: a thin layer of tomato sauce, eggplant slices, more tomato sauce, zucchini slices, an even layer of all the ricotta-pesto mixture, eggplant slices, more tomato sauce, zucchini slices, and the remaining tomato sauce. The last layer is the mozzarella, which should completely cover the top. Thin the remaining pesto with a bit of olive oil and brush on top of the mozzarella. Decoratively place the whole basil leaves on top of the pesto oil. Bake for 45 minutes. The mozzarella should be dark gold and the sauce bubbling around the sides of the dish. Let stand for a few minutes before cutting and serving.

GRILLED BUTTERFLIED LEG OF LAMB
WITH YOGURT-MINT SAUCE

Serves 10 to 12

Here's a good recipe to make to honor those days in mid-June, so long ago, when the entire Island population happily congregated to celebrate Sheep Shearing Day. While the roasted mutton that was offered for sale back then was probably prepared in a simpler way, this grilled leg of lamb, which combines the seasonings of islands in the Aegean Sea, will probably satisfy your sophisticated palate.

For the marinade

2 cups coarsely chopped fresh mint leaves

1 cup coarsely chopped fresh flat-leaf parsley

1 cup coarsely chopped yellow onion

3 cloves garlic, finely minced

1 tablespoon freshly ground black pepper

Grated zest and juice of 3 lemons

1 cup ouzo or another licorice-flavored liqueur such as Pernod or Ricard

½ cup extra-virgin olive oil

1 tablespoon kosher salt, or to taste

For the lamb

1 boneless leg of lamb, about 8 pounds, cleaned and butterflied

For the sauce

2 cups plain, whole milk yogurt

½ cup finely chopped fresh mint leaves

2 teaspoons paprika

Grated zest and juice of 1 lemon

1 teaspoon salt

1. Make the marinade: In a bowl, combine all of the ingredients.

2. Prepare the lamb: Place in a nonreactive baking dish. Rub the marinade on the surfaces of the lamb. Marinate for at least 4 hours, at room temperature, or up to 24 hours, in the refrigerator. Bring to room temperature 2 hours before grilling.

3. Make the sauce: In a bowl, combine all the ingredients. Whisk to mix well. Refrigerate until ready for use.

4. Start a fire in a grill. Grill the lamb for a total of about 30 minutes, turning every 10 minutes, until the interior temperature in the center reaches 135°F on an instant-read thermometer inserted into the thickest part. Let stand for 10 minutes, then divide the leg into shank sections before carving. Slice each section across the grain. Serve with the yogurt-mint sauce.

SUMMER VEGETABLE-GARDEN CURRY

Serves 10 to 12

This curry has it all—and I don't mean just the vegetables. The curry spices spark the vegetables, while the yogurt softens the strength of the seasonings and the lemon brightens it all. Don't let the abundant produce confuse you the next time you pass one of the Island's packed farm stands or when everything in your own garden ripens at once. Just buy or pick a little of everything, and make this curry. I like spicy curry, so I use 1 teaspoon ground cayenne pepper.

This recipe makes a large quantity. Curry, as with most other stews, becomes more flavorful a day later. Serve it on a bed of rice with a poached egg on top—what a lunch!

1 pound eggplant, cut into $^1/_2$-inch cubes

Salt, as needed

1 pound green, yellow, and red bell peppers, about 1 each, quartered

1 cup finely chopped yellow onion

1 large clove garlic, finely minced

2 teaspoons grated fresh ginger

1 teaspoon ground turmeric

1 teaspoon ground coriander

1 teaspoon ground cumin

$^1/_2$ teaspoon ground cayenne pepper

1 teaspoon fennel seeds

$^1/_2$ cup corn oil

2 pounds plum tomatoes, peeled and diced

Grated zest and juice of 1 lemon

1 teaspoon salt

1 cup water

$^1/_2$ pound green beans, vine ends removed, cut into 2-inch pieces

1 pound zucchini, cut into $^1/_2$-inch slices

$^1/_2$ pound chard, center ribs removed and torn into 2- to 3-inch pieces

$1^1/_2$ cups plain whole milk yogurt

1. Salt the eggplant, place in a colander, cover with paper towels, and weight with a heavy object such as a cast-iron skillet. Let drain for 30 minutes. Rinse and pat dry. Cut each pepper quarter into 1-inch strips. Make diagonal cuts on each strip 1 inch apart to form triangles.

2. In a 4-quart, heavy-bottomed saucepan over medium heat, sauté the onion, garlic, ginger, turmeric, coriander, cumin, cayenne, and fennel seeds in the corn oil. When the onion is soft, add the tomatoes and lemon zest and juice and stir until incorporated. Add the 1 teaspoon salt and the water.

3. Add the green beans, eggplant cubes, zucchini slices, and bell pepper triangles, one at a time, carefully folding them into the curry. Reduce the heat and simmer, covered, for 30 minutes, or until the vegetables are soft and permeated with curry spices. Add the chard and yogurt, and simmer, covered, for 15 minutes more. Serve hot or at room temperature.

FRAGRANT COUSCOUS WITH ROASTED AUTUMN VEGETABLES

Serves 6

While the Summer Vegetable-Garden Curry helps you solve the problem of which vegetables to choose for dinner from the Island's August harvest, this recipe for roasted vegetables gives you the same help when confronted with October's collection.

For the couscous

8 cups water

1 cinnamon stick

1 teaspoon cardamom pods

1/2 teaspoon whole cloves

2 bay leaves

2 teaspoons salt

2 tablespoons corn oil

2 cups regular couscous

1/4 cup dried currants

2 tablespoons toasted pine nuts

For the roasted vegetables

Salt, as needed

1 large eggplant, cut into 1/4-inch slices

2 pounds beets, peeled and cut into quarters or eighths

2 pounds turnips, peeled and cut into quarters or eighths

2 pounds carrots, peeled and cut into 2-inch pieces

1 butternut squash, 1 to 2 pounds, halved, peeled, seeded, and cut into 1 1/2-inch pieces

1 large bunch broccoli, cut into florets

2 red bell peppers, quartered

Olive oil, as needed

1. Make a broth for the couscous by combining the water, cinnamon stick, cardamom, cloves, bay leaves, and salt in a large saucepan. Simmer for 30 to 45 minutes. Preheat an oven to 500°F.

2. Prepare the vegetables: Salt the eggplant, place in a colander, cover with paper towels, and weight with a heavy object such as a cast-iron skillet. Let drain for 30 minutes. Rinse and pat dry.

3. Some of the vegetables should be roasted separately because they have different cooking times. The beets, turnips, carrots, and squash can be roasted together. Then roast separately, in this order, the broccoli, eggplant, and bell peppers. Arrange the vegetables in each batch on a baking sheet. Add a splash or two of olive oil and a sprinkling of salt. Use your hands to coat the vegetables completely with the oil and salt. Roast for 5 to 12 minutes, until the sides are crisp and the center is soft, turning once or twice during the cooking time. Peel the skin from the roasted peppers, then julienne them.

4. Make the couscous: Remove the spices from the broth. Put the corn oil and couscous in a heavy-bottomed skillet over medium heat and begin to stir. The couscous will immediately start to toast. As soon as most of it is toasted, begin to add the simmering broth 1 cup at a time, stirring constantly. As each addition is absorbed, add more broth. The couscous is done when the grains are tender but not soft. Add the currants with the last cup of broth. Stir the toasted pine nuts into the finished couscous.

5. Mound the couscous onto a warm serving dish. Arrange all the roasted vegetables except the julienned red bell pepper around the couscous. Garnish the couscous with the red pepper and serve.

Note: For the currants and pine nuts used in the couscous, you may prefer to substitute apricots and pistachios or prunes and walnuts.

S|

&

CHAPTER FOUR

DE DISHES
VEGETABLES

SICILIAN RICE SALAD

Serves 6

One glorious August morning, as I softly swayed in my hammock under a bright blue Quidnet sky, my thoughts drifted to a simple question: What brilliant person wrote the first recipe? My research showed that the first book of recipes was written in the fifth century B.C. in the Sicilian town of Siracusa by a Greek colonist called Mithaecus. The colonist's passion for cooking was the direct result of the uncommon abundance of raw ingredients growing on the island and being caught in the surrounding sea. The star of this book, another island, an ocean away from Sicily, also enjoys an abundance of ingredients. I've borrowed the pine nuts, currants, bread crumbs, and vinegar from Sicily and added them to the ingredients of Nantucket's summer. The dish created does both islands proud.

1/2 pound chard, cut into ribbons as for Egg-Lemon Soup (page 42)

1/2 cup water

3/4 pound sugar snap peas, strings removed

1/3 cup dried currants

1/4 cup pine nuts

1/2 cup toasted unseasoned bread crumbs

1/4 cup extra-virgin olive oil

1 tablespoon red wine vinegar

Salt and freshly ground pepper

1 cup converted rice, cooked, drained, and cooled

1. Put the chard ribbons and 1/2 cup water in a heavy-bottomed skillet over medium heat, cover, and steam the chard until tender, 5 to 7 minutes. Drain and let cool. Fill a saucepan with water and bring to a boil. Blanch the peas for 15 seconds. Plunge into ice water to halt the cooking, and drain on paper towels.

2. In a bowl, combine the chard, sugar snap peas, currants, pine nuts, half of the toasted bread crumbs, olive oil, vinegar, salt, and pepper with the cooked rice.

3. To serve, sprinkle the remaining bread crumbs over the rice salad.

WEDDING DAY RICE

Serves 6

Traditionally, newlyweds are showered with rice as they leave the church as a way of wishing them good fortune. Continued good fortune will be theirs if a rice dish like this one is served at their reception. Because I'm particularly partial to rice, a tender, juice-absorbing grain, I use it as often as possible. This rice recipe, studded with the vegetables of the June harvest, is perfectly suited to sit alongside chicken, fish, beef, or lamb.

Wedding Day Rice owes its origins to the first June wedding that I catered over fifteen years ago. It's so good that I've made it ever since for all early summer celebrations. Follow the Nantucket harvest and create your own rice dishes by combining vegetables, herbs, cheese, and nuts. I'm sure good fortune will be yours!

$1/2$ cup shelled, tiny new peas (a little more than $1/2$ pound in the shells)

$3/4$ cup thinly sliced radishes

2 cucumbers, peeled, seeded, and finely diced

2 tablespoons finely chopped fresh dill

$1/2$ cup crumbled feta cheese

Grated zest and juice of 1 lemon

$1/2$ cup toasted and chopped walnuts

2 tablespoons extra-virgin olive oil

1 teaspoon salt

$1^{1}/2$ cups basmati or converted rice, cooked, drained, and cooled

1. Fill a saucepan with water and bring to a boil. Blanch the peas in the boiling water for 2 minutes to bring up their color. Plunge into a bowl of ice water to halt the cooking, and drain on paper towels.

2. In a bowl, combine the radishes, cucumbers, dill, feta, lemon zest and juice, walnuts, olive oil, and salt with the rice. Toss to mix well. Serve at room temperature.

CORN THAT'S JUST RIGHT

I f we sell today's corn tomorrow, it's yesterday's corn. We're too small to lose a customer because of quality." That's Steve Slosek of Moors End Farm telling me exactly how fresh the corn is at his Polpis Road stand. "It has to be picked properly, at just the right time—and often." Some call Slosek's corn "underdone," because he picks it young and rather green. I call it just right, sweet, crisp and full of flavor without a hint of starch. Steve jokes that if the corn at the stand is two hours old, it's thrown away. That's not the case, but the truth in his exaggeration lies in the fact that about 90 percent of the sugar in corn starts to turn to starch within hours of picking.

Don't be afraid to ask when the corn you're about to purchase was picked. Even better, find out when the next batch of newly picked corn will arrive at the stand. At that point, buy several dozen. Use some immediately for the two recipes here. Then either roast the remaining ears as for Roasted Corn Soup (page 51) and scrape the kernels off the cob, or scrape raw kernels off the cob and freeze the roasted or raw kernels in a labeled container. This most popular of all vegetables will be on hand as a surprise ingredient for a wintertime meal.

CARROT-CORN SAFFRON RICE

Serves 6

This saffron-tinted rice is the perfect accompaniment to spicy summer fish like Grilled Whole Bluefish (page 72) when all the ingredients are summertime fresh.

- 1½ quarts water
- ½ teaspoon saffron threads
- 2 new onions, thinly sliced
- 2 tablespoons corn oil
- 4 carrots, shredded
- Kernels from 4 ears of corn
- 1 cup basmati rice
- ½ cup coarsely chopped fresh cilantro
- Salt

1. In a saucepan, boil the water and saffron, reduce the heat and simmer, cover askew, for 45 minutes, to color and flavor the cooking water for the rice.

2. In a skillet over medium heat, sauté the onions in the corn oil until transparent. Add the carrots, stir to combine with the onions, and cook for 5 minutes, or until the carrots are tender and the onions are translucent. Add the corn and cook for 3 minutes. Remove from the heat and let cool.

3. Cook the rice in the saffron water over medium heat, cover askew, until tender but not soft, 10 to 12 minutes. Drain and let cool.

4. In a bowl, mix the vegetables and cilantro with the rice. Season to taste with salt. I purposely leave out pepper because this dish is usually served with a spicy main course. Serve at room temperature.

WHEATBERRY SUCCOTASH

Serves 6

I can't find the facts to back me up, but I'd like to think that when Thomas Macy brought the first group of English settlers to Nantucket in 1659, one of the things in his wife's possession was a recipe for succotash. Originally this hearty, life-sustaining mix consisted of white beans, corn, turnips, potatoes, whole chicken, pork, and corned beef—a recipe still used to celebrate Forefather's Day every December 22 in Plymouth, Massachusetts. Known to the colonists by the Narragansett Indian name, msickquatash, *succotash now needs contain only a mixture of corn and lima beans to be considered authentic.*

My succotash, which is made with tender young lima beans, sweet corn kernels, crisp bacon bits, raw onion, and parsley combined with nutty wheatberries, pays homage to the original, more substantial version. It can be made year-round using beans and corn you have frozen from the summer harvest.

1 cup wheatberries

Kernels from 3 ears of corn

1 cup baby lima beans

¼ pound smoked bacon

1 rounded tablespoon finely chopped yellow onion

2 tablespoons finely chopped, fresh flat-leaf parsley

2 teaspoons red wine vinegar

1 teaspoon salt

Freshly ground black pepper

1. In a bowl, soak the wheatberries in water to cover for at least 2 hours or up to 12 hours. Cook in abundant water over medium heat, uncovered, until tender, 1 to 1½ hours. Dice the bacon and fry in a skillet over low heat until very crispy. Drain on paper towels.

2. Blanch the lima beans and corn kernels in a saucepan of boiling water. Cook for about 3 minutes. Plunge into ice water to halt cooking and drain on paper towels.

3. In a bowl, combine the beans, corn, bacon, onion, parsley, vinegar, salt and pepper to taste with the cooled wheatberries. Serve at room temperature.

POTATO AND TOMATO SALAD

Serves 6

The inspiration for this salad comes from a recipe made for me by a friend who has a vacation home on the island of Pantelleria. Pantelleria, off the coast of Sicily and very close to Africa, is home to world-famous capers that thrive in the volcanic soil under the hot sun. With two jars of salt-preserved capers from my friend's property, and his recipe lodged in my mind, I transported them to Nantucket, where they are suited to the superb tomatoes and delicious new potatoes that arrive at farm stands at about the same time. The classic version of this salad includes a tiny fish found only near Pantelleria. I've substituted Nantucket's own smoked bluefish instead.

1½ pounds new potatoes, cut into ½-inch pieces

1 pound tomatoes, seeded and coarsely chopped

¼ cup finely diced red onion

½ cup finely flaked smoked bluefish or any other available smoked fish

2 tablespoons salt-preserved capers, rinsed

½ cup firmly packed, coarsely chopped fresh flat-leaf parsley

½ cup extra-virgin olive oil

¼ pound dense Mediterranean bread, soaked in water for 15 minutes and squeezed dry

Salt

1. Cook the potatoes in abundant boiling water until a tester easily passes through them. Drain and plunge into ice water to halt the cooking. Dry on paper towels.

2. In a bowl, combine the potatoes, tomatoes, onion, bluefish, capers, parsley, and olive oil. Crumble the dried bread and add to the mixture. Taste for salt and add as needed; the bluefish and capers are salty. Serve at room temperature.

THE BEST WILD RICE

Serves 6

Wild rice is not a true rice, but the seed of an aquatic plant. Harvested for centuries by the Chippewa Indians of the Great Lakes region, the wild, grassy plants grow in the water as true rice grows in a paddy. Because wild rice insinuates itself so gracefully with such Nantucket ingredients as cranberries and pumpkins, fish, and game, I sometimes forget that it doesn't actually grow here. This version of wild rice is my standard. I serve it hot the first time, then at room temperature, or I mix an egg in it and make little croquettes that are sautéed and served with cocktails.

1½ cups wild rice

2 carrots, peeled and finely diced

2 celery ribs, finely diced

1 yellow onion, finely diced

2 tablespoons unsalted butter

1 cup orange juice

½ cup dry white vermouth

2½ cups vegetable broth (page 44)

2 tablespoons pure olive oil

¼ cup dried currants

½ cup pecan pieces

4 scallions, both white and green parts, coarsely chopped

1. In a bowl, soak the rice in abundant water, uncovered, at room temperature, overnight. Drain.

2. In a skillet over medium heat, sauté the carrots, celery, and onion in the butter and I tablespoon of the olive oil for about 5 minutes. Add the rice and thoroughly combine. Cover the mixture with the orange juice, vermouth, and vegetable broth. Simmer over low heat until the rice is cooked to your preference, 45 to 60 minutes. With the heat very low, add the currants.

3. In a small skillet over medium heat, sauté the pecan pieces in the remaining I tablespoon olive oil. As soon as the nuts start to toast, add the scallions. Stir once or twice to combine. Add to the wild rice and combine. Serve hot or at room temperature.

Lentils and Spinach with Cumin-Onion Vinaigrette

Serves 4

I like to serve this combination with Summertime Codfish Cakes (page 66), to offer a new twist on an old standard—beans and cod. Fresh spinach is available all spring and is planted again at the end of summer for a fall harvest. In Nantucket, which almost always has cool summer nights, it's possible to find fresh local spinach for at least five months of the year.

1 yellow onion, thinly sliced
2 pounds spinach, stems removed
1 tablespoon balsamic vinegar
1 tablespoon lemon juice
1 teaspoon grated lemon zest
1 teaspoon ground cumin
3 tablespoons extra-virgin olive oil
Salt and freshly ground white pepper
2 cups cooked lentils

1. Soak the onion slices in a bowl of salted ice water for 1 hour. This will take out some of the sting associated with raw onions. Squeeze with your hands to remove the water.

2. Put the spinach in a heavy, nonreactive skillet over low heat with 2 to 3 tablespoons water, cover and steam for 5 minutes. Remove from the heat, drain, and let cool.

3. In a bowl, combine the vinegar, lemon juice and zest, and cumin. Slowly add the oil, stirring with a small whisk or fork to achieve a good tight emulsion. Season to taste with salt and pepper; the onions will contribute a fair amount of salt. Add the onions to the vinaigrette.

4. In a bowl, toss together the lentils and spinach. Top with the vinaigrette and onions. Let stand for 15 minutes or so before serving at room temperature.

GRILLED EGGPLANT ROLLS WITH RAW TOMATO SAUCE

Makes 16 rolls

When I called my sister Laura to ask her to help me come up with a Nantucket eggplant anecdote, she just happened to be in her potting shed transplanting eggplant seedlings. Laura grows two varieties of purple-skinned eggplant: Ichiban, a Japanese eggplant, and the very familiar Black Beauty. These two sturdy-skinned eggplants are perfect for grilling and roasting. Bartlett's Ocean View Farm has recently begun to grow a variety of the softer-skinned, white eggplant. While it's equally as tasty as the purple-skinned-eggplant, it's more appropriate for baking and frying. I suggest that you choose two shiny, deep purple, Black Beauty eggplants and then make these savory grilled eggplant rolls.

For the eggplant

2 medium to large eggplants

Salt

2 pounds fresh spinach, stems removed

$1/2$ cup crumbled feta cheese

$1/4$ cup dried currants

2 tablespoons pine nuts

2 tablespoons pure olive oil

Grated zest and juice of 1 lemon

Freshly ground white pepper

For the tomato sauce

4 large or 6 medium vine-ripened tomatoes

$1/2$ cup fresh basil leaves

1 large clove garlic, finely minced

2 tablespoons extra-virgin olive oil

1. Prepare the eggplant rolls: Cut the eggplants lengthwise into $1/4$-inch slices; you should have at least 16 slices. Layer the slices in a colander, salt every other layer, put a paper towel over the last layer and weight the eggplant with a heavy object such as a cast-iron skillet. Let drain for 30 minutes.

2. In a nonreactive saucepan over low heat, steam the spinach with 2 tablespoons water until wilted. Let cool. In a bowl, combine the spinach, feta, and currants.

3. In a small skillet over medium heat, cook the pine nuts in the olive oil until they begin to smell like popcorn, then *immediately*——they will over overcook in a split second—pour over the spinach mixture. Add lemon zest and juice. Add pepper to taste. Salt to taste, but bear in mind the saltiness of the feta and the eggplant slices.

4. Start a fire in a grill. Rinse and dry the eggplant. Grill for about 2 minutes on each side, or until slightly golden. Alternatively, grill on an indoor stovetop grill or cook over high heat in a cast-iron skillet, for about 2 minutes on each side. Let cool for just a few minutes.

5. Lay out the slices on a work surface. Place several tablespoons of the spinach filling at the wide end of each slice. Roll toward the narrow end. To hold the roll together, place with narrow end down on a platter.

6. Make the tomato sauce: Plunge the tomatoes in boiling water for a few seconds, just enough to loosen the skins. Peel, remove the seeds, and coarsely chop. Make a chiffonade of the basil: Neatly pile a group of leaves together, roll tightly, and thinly slice. Repeat until all the basil has been sliced. In a bowl, combine the tomatoes, basil, garlic, and oil. Add salt to taste, bearing in mind that the sauce will be served with the seasoned eggplant rolls.

7. Serve the rolls at room temperature with the sauce.

SUGAR SNAP PEAS WITH MUSTARD OIL–ORANGE VINAIGRETTE

Serves 4 to 6

Nantucket's sugar snap peas, as sweet and crunchy as their name implies, have met their perfect match in mustard oil, an improbable alliance to say the least. Pungent, sharp mustard oil is a condiment used almost exclusively in the kitchens of India, a country where sugar snaps don't even grow. It is a dish where opposites attract, with the orange acting as the matchmaker. I like to garnish the peas with thin orange slices.

1½ pounds sugar snap peas, strings removed
¼ cup orange juice
1 tablespoon grated orange zest
2 teaspoons sherry vinegar
2 teaspoons crushed pink peppercorns
Salt
2 tablespoons mustard oil

1. Blanch the sugar snap peas in a saucepan of boiling water for 15 seconds. Plunge into ice water to halt the cooking. Drain on paper towels.

2. In a bowl, combine the orange juice and zest, vinegar, peppercorns, and salt to taste, slowly add the mustard oil, stirring with a small whisk or fork in order to achieve a good, tight emulsion.

3. Combine the peas and vinaigrette. Place on platter garnished with orange slices and serve at room temperature.

PEPERONATA

Serves 8

At the end of the summer, right through October, you see mountains of green, red, and yellow bell peppers in green markets and at farm stands. Buy them by the pounds, take them home, and make lots of peperonata. This is another dish that ripens and improves after a couple of days in the refrigerator. While the color of the peperonata will fade slightly, the flavor will not. Serve peperonata as the vegetable course with dinner, fold it into an omelette, use it as a condiment on a sandwich, toss it with pasta —you get the idea. It will keep for a week, if it lasts that long.

1 cup thinly sliced yellow onions

$1/2$ cup pure olive oil

1 tablespoon fresh thyme leaves

$1/2$ teaspoon finely minced fresh hot pepper such as
    Thai, cayenne, or red jalapeño

3 green bell peppers, cut into $1/2$-inch strips

3 red bell peppers, cut into $1/2$-inch strips

3 yellow bell peppers, cut into $1/2$-inch strips

1 tablespoon anchovy paste

1. In a large heavy-bottomed, nonreactive pot over medium heat, sauté the onions in the olive oil until soft. Add the thyme and hot pepper, then the bell peppers. Stir thoroughly to combine. Add the anchovy paste, and stir to combine with the peppers.

2. Lower the heat a notch and simmer, cover askew, until the peppers are soft but not mushy, about 30 minutes. Let stand a bit before serving.

ZUCCHINI POSING AS FETTUCCINE WITH LEMON CREAM

Serves 6

My friend Helen Potter loves words as much as she loves food. Faced with a bumper crop of zucchini—sound familiar?—she rhymed zucchini with fettuccine and came up with this way to serve the slender green squash. The lemon cream sauce is mine, but any silky sauce will do: tomato cream, fresh tomato (page 131), olive oil and garlic.

1 cup heavy cream
6 tender young zucchini, 6 to 7 inches long
1 rounded tablespoon grated Parmesan cheese
Grated zest of 1 lemon
Juice of 1/2 lemon
1 tablespoon finely chopped fresh chives
Salt and freshly ground white pepper

1. Put the cream in a small, heavy-bottomed saucepan and simmer to reduce by half, about 30 to 40 minutes. Cut the ends off the zucchini. Using a vegetable peeler, cut each zucchini into lengthwise strips. Bring a large saucepan of water to a boil.

2. Add the Parmesan and lemon zest to the reduced cream. Stir to combine and simmer until the zucchini is peeled. Add the zucchini strips to the boiling water, stir a few times, and cook for 2 minutes. Drain well. In a large bowl, toss with the lemon juice.

3. Add the chives to the lemon cream and pour over the zucchini. Add salt and pepper to taste. Serve hot or at room temperature.

SAUTÉED KALE WITH HOT PEPPERS AND GARLIC

Serves 4

Kale, a member of the brassica, or cabbage, family, grows well near the sea, in cool climates. This makes it the dominant green on Nantucket's farm stands, from Indian summer through the winter. After the first frost, it's the remaining visible crop in the Island's private gardens. I'm always amused to see the sturdy dark green leaves supporting mounds of snow. Kale needs to be combined with other strong ingredients that emphasize the flavor. The Portuguese population of southern New England moistens and spices it in this simple preparation.

2 cloves garlic, finely minced
1/4 cup extra-virgin olive oil
2 pounds kale, stemmed and torn into 2-inch pieces
1/2 teaspoon fresh hot pepper such as Thai or cayenne, finely minced
1 teaspoon kosher salt
Optional: good-quality red wine vinegar

1. In a large, heavy-bottomed skillet over medium heat, sauté the garlic in the olive oil. When the garlic is golden, add the kale, two handfuls at a time, waiting for it to wilt slightly between additions. Add the hot pepper and salt.

2. Reduce the heat to low and cook until the kale is tender, 3 to 4 minutes. Taste for salt. Sprinkle with vinegar if desired. Serve immediately.

CHOPPED VEGETABLE SALAD WITH TURMERIC AND FENNEL DRIZZLE

Serves 6

This mosaic of summer vegetables wrapped in yogurt, then painted with a golden turmeric drizzle, is the summer salad that I love best. The combination of flavors, textures, and colors is sensational. Nantucket's vine-ripened, still-warm-from-the-sun tomatoes make this already exciting salad heavenly.

3 large tomatoes, seeded and diced

2 cucumbers, peeled, seeded, and diced

1 green bell pepper, finely diced

3 scallions, white and green parts, thinly sliced

1 cup plain, whole milk yogurt

1 teaspoon salt

$\frac{1}{2}$ teaspoon freshly ground black pepper

3 tablespoons pure olive oil

1 teaspoon fennel seeds

1 teaspoon ground turmeric

1. In a bowl, combine the tomatoes, cucumbers, bell pepper, and scallions with the yogurt, salt, and pepper. Put in a serving dish.

2. Heat the olive oil in a small skillet over medium heat. Add the fennel seeds, and when they begin to pop, add the turmeric. Stir 3 or 4 times and remove from the heat. Drizzle over the salad and serve immediately.

Note: The chopped vegetables and yogurt may be combined ahead of time and refrigerated. The drizzle can then be made just before serving.

ROASTED SWEET POTATOES, CORN, AND RED PEPPERS

Serves 6

I once served this dish at Thanksgiving dinner using Moor's End Farm corn that had been frozen for fourteen months. It was the most applauded dish on the menu. Freezing a vegetable for so long is very, very chancy (it tends to dehydrate). I got lucky that time. You can feel safe using frozen summer corn for the following winter and spring.

2 pounds sweet potatoes
2 red bell peppers
Kernels from 4 ears of corn
Corn oil for coating vegetables
6 thyme sprigs, plus sprigs for garnish
1½ teaspoons kosher salt
Freshly ground pepper

1. Preheat an oven to 500° F. Bring a saucepan of water to a boil. Cut the potatoes into 2-inch pieces. Cook in the boiling water for about 5 minutes. Drain and let cool. Roast the whole bell peppers over a gas flame, turning until completely charred. Put in a bowl, and seal with plastic wrap, and keep covered for at least 30 minutes. Alternatively, roast in a preheated 450° F oven: Cut the peppers in half, coat with corn oil, place on a baking sheet skin-side down, and roast until charred, about 20 minutes. Peel the skin from the peppers, discard the seeds and membranes, and cut into ¼-inch strips.

2. Roast the corn kernels on a baking sheet for 10 minutes in the 500° F oven. Turn with a spatula after 5 minutes.

3. Cut the potatoes into 1-inch pieces. Coat with corn oil. Toss with the 6 thyme sprigs and salt and a few twists of pepper. Place on a baking sheet and roast until slightly browned, 20 to 25 minutes, turning every 7 minutes so that most of the sides get crunchy.

4. In a bowl, toss the corn, potatoes, and half of the roasted peppers together. Most of the thyme leaves will have fallen off the sprigs during the roasting; remove the twigs. Serve hot or at room temperature garnished with the remaining roasted peppers and thyme sprigs.

BUTTERNUT SQUASH GRATIN

Serves 6

Check out the local farm stands in late September. Like Henry Moore sculptures of the vegetable world, butternut squash are displayed at the autumn show of the Museum of Nantucket Vegetables. Their bright orange flesh is as tasty as their butterscotch good looks are sensual.

- 1 butternut squash, about 3 pounds, peeled, seeded, and cut into 1-inch cubes
- 1 yellow onion, thinly sliced
- 1 tablespoon pure olive oil
- 2 tablespoons unsalted butter
- 1/2 cup heavy cream
- 8 fresh sage leaves
- 1 large egg, slightly beaten
- 1/4 teaspoon freshly grated nutmeg
- 1/4 teaspoon freshly ground white pepper
- 1 teaspoon salt
- 2 tablespoons grated Parmesan cheese

1. Put the squash cubes on a steamer rack set in a saucepan of water simmering over medium heat. Steam until tender, about 15 minutes.

2. In a skillet over medium heat, sauté the onion in the olive oil until caramel colored and crispy. In a saucepan over medium heat, melt the 2 tablespoons butter, and add the cream and sage leaves. Lower the heat a notch and simmer for 10 to 15 minutes.

3. Preheat an oven to 350°F. Purée the squash in a blender or food processor. Remove the sage leaves from the cream and reserve. Add the onion, cream, egg, nutmeg, pepper, and salt to the purée, and stir to combine. Pour into a buttered gratin dish. Attractively arrange the cream-coated sage leaves on top of the squash. Sprinkle with the Parmesan cheese. Bake until the top is golden, 45 minutes. Serve immediately.

D
C
&

CHAPTER FIVE

RESSINGS, ONDIMENTS, SAUCES

Salads and Salad Dressings

Salads as we know them were not common on Nantucket until a few decades into the twentieth century. While Islanders were fond of pickling the odd cucumber or onion, lettuce salads weren't served and the crop wasn't cultivated. When salads finally became a menu item, dressings tended to mimic pickling methods, and lettuce was coated with sugar, salt, and vinegar.

Now that salad is the food of the twentieth century, Nantucket farmers are accommodating the consuming public with greater varieties of leaves, herbs, and even flowers to enable the construction of more elaborate and tantalizing salads. Bartlett's Ocean View Farm grows mesclun and edible flowers, and Moors End Farm grows the much-loved (and rare on the East Coast) Bibb lettuce, which disappears from the claw-footed bathtub where it's displayed as quickly as it's put there. The Island is also home to a few commercial gardens that grow a wide variety of herbs sold in pots and bunches. Some of the businesses also make vinegars infused with their herbs. These products, like the greater selection of greens, are made to satisfy the demand for interesting and varied salad ingredients.

Two-Mustard Vinaigrette

Makes 1 cup

This is the vinaigrette that I use more than any other. It's all-purpose. Because it's full of flavor in a nonintrusive way, it works well with a soft buttery lettuce like Boston or a limestone like Bibb, as well as with stronger, more peppery leaves like watercress or arugula.

I use pure olive oil for vinaigrettes and dressings that include other ingredients with strong flavors like mustard—extra-virgin olive oil would be too competitive in a vinaigrette like this one or the Ginger Vinaigrette (page 127).

1 tablespoon Dijon mustard
1 tablespoon whole-grain mustard such as Moutard de Meaux
2 teaspoons sherry vinegar
1 teaspoon kosher salt
1 cup pure olive oil
Freshly ground black pepper

1. In a small bowl, mix the mustards, vinegar, and salt.

2. Slowly whisk in the olive oil to create a smooth, creamy emulsion. Add pepper to taste. The vinaigrette can be stored for up to 4 weeks, refrigerated, in a jar with a tight-fitting lid. Whisk before serving.

GINGER VINAIGRETTE

Makes 1¼ cups

I use this dressing for salads that are combinations of quickly blanched vegetables or for simple, single-vegetable cold dishes. The dressing is splendid with snow peas, sugar snap peas, green beans, carrots, and, my favorite, asparagus.

1 rounded tablespoon grated fresh ginger
1 tablespoon Dijon mustard
1 teaspoon powdered Chinese mustard
1 tablespoon soy sauce
Grated zest and juice of 1 small lime
2 teaspoons rice vinegar
1 cup pure olive oil

1. In a small bowl, mix the ginger, Dijon mustard, Chinese mustard, soy sauce, lime zest and juice, and rice vinegar.

2. Slowly whisk in the olive oil to create a smooth creamy emulsion. The vinaigrette can be stored for up to 2 weeks, refrigerated, in a jar with a tight-fitting lid. Whisk before serving.

CREAMY PARMESAN AND GARLIC DRESSING

Makes 1⅓ cups

This is a great dressing for composed or mixed salads. Lettuce, tomatoes, cucumbers, radishes, peppers, and scallions—sort of a tossed antipasto—served with some hard-cooked eggs and a few good olives, make the best summer supper.

1 egg yolk
2 rounded tablespoons grated Parmesan cheese
1 clove garlic, thinly sliced
1 teaspoon dried oregano
1 tablespoon white wine vinegar
1¼ cups extra-virgin olive oil
Salt and freshly ground black pepper

1. Place the egg yolk, cheese, garlic, oregano, and vinegar in a food processor. Process for a few seconds to combine the ingredients.

2. With the machine on, slowly dribble in the olive oil and process until the dressing is creamy. Taste for salt and pepper and add as desired. The dressing can be stored for up to 2 weeks, refrigerated, in a jar with a tight-fitting lid. Shake before serving.

MAPLE SYRUP CRÈME ANGLAISE

Makes 2½ cups

One of the items offered for sale at the Moors End Farm stand is Vermont pure maple syrup—heaven on earth! The Sloseks, who own the farm, winter in Vermont and are connected to that state's maple syrup industry. Steve Slosek and I disagree rather passionately about which grade of syrup tastes better. Steve, an assimilated Vermonter, takes the position that most natives do: use Fancy Grade A or nothing. I, on the other hand, am crazy about the thick, intensely flavored Grade B.

I say make this Maple Syrup Crème Anglaise with Grade B syrup if possible. This sauce works wonderfully well with warm fruit cobblers and crisps, fresh berries, and fruit salads.

1¾ cups heavy cream
2 large egg yolks
¾ cup Grade B maple syrup

1. In a heavy-bottomed saucepan over medium heat, scald the cream. In a bowl, whisk the egg yolks into the maple syrup to combine completely. Remove the scalded cream from the heat. Add the syrup mixture to the cream. Stir to combine.

2. Place the sauce over low heat (higher heat will scramble the eggs), and stir constantly with a wooden spoon. Make sure that you move the spoon in all directions along the bottom of the pan. The sauce will thicken as it cooks. When it coats the back of the spoon and doesn't run off immediately, it's ready. Serve hot, at room temperature, or chilled. The sauce can be stored in the refrigerator for up to 4 days.

SESAME CREAM FOR BITTER GREENS

Makes ½ cup, enough for 1 pound of greens

Today we live in a global economy. When it's wintertime in the United States, just turn the earth upside down and shake, and the most wonderful summertime crops will come tumbling your way from South America and Australia. This means that there are wonderful salad choices the year round. I adore chicory and escarole, usually overlooked as too bitter to eat raw. But when covered with this rich, sweet, and nutty sesame cream, the greens become a kind of digestif or dessert—all the more reason to serve the salad, European style, after the main course.

Of course, the most crisp, most vitamin A-filled chicory and escarole grow in Nantucket's invariably cool-in-the-evening climate.

⅓ cup heavy cream
1 teaspoon sherry vinegar
1 tablespoon Asian sesame oil
1 tablespoon pure honey
½ teaspoon salt
1 teaspoon soy sauce
1 rounded teaspoon sour cream
Freshly ground white pepper

1. In a small bowl, whisk together all the ingredients to combine fully. Use immediately.

FRESH FRUIT CHUTNEY

Makes about 6 cups

Inspired by the simple chutneys of the Seychelles Islands in the Indian Ocean, this one is made with a mixture of summer fruits and is the perfect accompaniment for just about any fish, fowl, meat, or grain dish that you might prepare. By the way, because there was a whale-processing plant on one of the smaller islands of the Seychelles, Nantucket whalers were regular visitors. Check out the display in the Nantucket Whaling Museum that features some of the souvenirs that these men brought home.

2 red onions, thinly sliced

3 large peaches, peeled, pitted, and diced

1 small cantaloupe, peeled, seeded, and diced

3 Granny Smith apples, cored and diced

1/2 cup coarsely chopped fresh cilantro leaves

1/2 cup dried currants or raisins

1/3 cup finely julienned crystallized ginger

1/4 cup pure olive oil

2 fresh hot peppers such as jalapeño, Thai, or
    cayenne, finely minced

Salt

1. Soak the onions in a bowl of salted ice water for 1 hour. This will remove some of the bite associated with raw onions.

2. Squeeze the onions dry with your hands. In a bowl, combine the onions with the remaining ingredients except the salt. Add salt to taste, bearing in mind that the onions are salty. The chutney lasts for up to a week when refrigerated. It may discolor a bit.

TARTAR SAUCE

Makes about 2 cups

This velvety smooth, slightly piquant mayonnaise with little sour surprises is the ideal condiment for salty foods that are crisp on the outside and sweet and soft on the inside. Fried clams aren't the same without tartar sauce. It's also the sauce of choice for fried fish. Try it as well with fried batter-dipped vegetables.

The obvious explanation for why it's called tartar sauce is that it contains the same ingredients used to make steak tartar. Quite honestly, I'd rather have this sauce with a grilled rare hamburger. I also like it mixed in potato salad.

1 large egg
1 tablespoon capers in vinegar
1/4 cup cornichons
Grated zest of 1 lemon
Pinch of ground cayenne pepper
1 1/2 cups corn oil
Salt
Optional: 1 tablespoon chopped fresh tarragon
    or dill

1. Place the egg and half of the capers and cornichons in a food processor. Process until the egg is pale and frothy. Stop the machine, and add the lemon zest, cayenne, and remaining capers and cornichons. With the machine running, slowly dribble in all of the corn oil until a tight mayonnaise is achieved. Taste for salt.

2. Remove from the food processor, and swirl in the fresh herbs if desired. Refrigerate the sauce until ready for use. It will keep for up to 3 weeks.

Note: The cornichon, literally "gherkin" in French, is a small, tart pickle about 2 inches long.

FRESH TOMATO SAUCE WITH VARIATIONS

Makes about 2 cups

This is my stock sauce; simple and direct. I use the late-summer bounty of Island tomatoes—so profuse and prized in Nantucket that Bartlett's Farm sponsors a "Great Tomato Cook-Off" recipe contest every August. I like to use a skillet rather than a saucepan to make the sauce. The wide opening allows the moisture to evaporate quickly and the sauce to concentrate more evenly.

1 clove garlic, finely minced

¼ cup pure olive oil

2 tablespoons unsalted butter

2 pounds plum tomatoes, peeled and coarsely chopped

Salt

Optional: 2 tablespoons chopped fresh herbs such as parsley, basil, mint, or dill

1. In a heavy-bottomed, nonreactive skillet over medium heat, sauté the garlic in the olive oil and butter for about 30 seconds. Simultaneously raise the heat and add the tomatoes.

2. Reduce the heat and simmer the sauce until it is reduced by one-third, 20 to 30 minutes. Add salt to taste and fresh herbs as desired. Let cool and refrigerate or freeze until ready for use. Refrigerated, it will keep for up to 2 weeks; frozen, it will keep for up to 1 year (until next year's summer tomato crop).

Variations:

With zucchini: Slice 2 slender zucchini on the diagonal. Sauté with the garlic for 3 minutes, stirring occasionally with a wooden spoon, before adding the tomatoes. Finish with 2 tablespoons chopped fresh basil.

With eggplant: Cut 1 small eggplant into ½ inch cubes, sprinkle with salt, place in a colander, cover with paper towels, and weight with a heavy object such as a cast-iron skillet. Let drain for 30 minutes. Rinse the cubes and pat dry. Sauté with the garlic for 3 to 4 minutes, stirring occasionally with a wooden spoon, before adding the tomatoes. Finish with 2 tablespoons chopped fresh flat-leaf parsley.

With lemon: Slice ½ lemon very, very thinly and remove the seeds. Add to the sauce after the tomatoes. Finish with 2 tablespoons chopped fresh mint.

CRANBERRIES ON NANTUCKET

Nantucket's Milestone cranberry bog is the world's largest contiguous natural bog." For years that's what I boasted to all who'd listen. It seems that I was mistaken, but only sort of. Until 1959, the bog that runs from the Milestone Road on the south to the Polpis Road on the north was a connected bog of cultivated cranberries. In order to conserve water, one of the Island's most precious resources, an intricate system of ditches and dikes now subdivides the bog. Though it is more water efficient, it is no longer entitled to the status of the world's largest.

In 1968, the bogs were purchased from the Nantucket Cranberry Co. by a group of preservation-minded gents, who in turn donated the land to the Nantucket Conservation Foundation. The foundation, which is dedicated to preserving and protecting the natural beauty of the Island, now leases about 260 acres of the bog to Northland Cranberries, Inc., which cultivates and harvests America's "first berry."

CRANBERRY-MANGO CHUTNEY

Makes about 4 cups

The Native Americans of southeastern Massachusetts used cranberries for everything from dyes to medicine and, most importantly, food. The native cranberry concoction was pemmican: cranberries pounded with animal fat, made into little cakes, and reserved for future consumption. The Native Americans also made wonderful cranberry sauces sweetened with maple syrup or honey to serve with fish, fowl, or meat. We all know when this sweet-tart sauce was first served and became forever associated with America's favorite holiday, Thanksgiving.

Cranberries are so highly acid that they practically self-preserve. To salute the ingeniousness of the Native Americans who sometimes preserved the berries and sometimes sweetened and cooked them for immediate consumption, I offer the East Indian method of pickling fruits and vegetables. I urge you to try this chutney with your next holiday bird.

- 1/2 cup Major Grey's chutney
- 1/4 cup cider vinegar
- 1/2 cup firmly packed brown sugar
- 1 cheesecloth bag holding 1 cinnamon stick (about 3 inches), 1/2 teaspoon whole cloves (about 8), and 1 piece fresh ginger (about 2 inches)
- 1 1/2 cups water
- 1/2 lime, blanched for 2 minutes and finely diced
- 1 firm pear, cored and finely diced
- 1 firm apple, cored and finely diced
- 3 cups cranberries
- 1/2 cup dried currants

1. In a large nonreactive saucepan, combine the chutney, vinegar, sugar, cheesecloth bag with spices, and water. Bring to a boil and stir until the sugar is dissolved. Add the lime, pear, and apple, reduce the heat, and simmer for 10 minutes.

2. Add the cranberries and currants, and simmer for 20 to 25 minutes, stirring occasionally. When the mixture is thick, remove from the heat and discard the cheesecloth bag.

3. Transfer to a glass or ceramic bowl. Let cool. Chill to allow flavors to blend before serving. The chutney can be stored in the refrigerator in a jar with a tight-fitting lid for up to 1 year.

D
&

CHAPTER SIX

ESSERTS
PASTRIES

TART LEMON TART

Serves 6 to 8

If the Minister of Desserts suddenly decided that every citizen were allowed to choose only one dessert for life, I'd pick this lemon tart. That's how strongly I feel about it. It's got all the ingredients and textures that I adore: a flaky, crunchy crust filled with a satiny smooth, buttery, sweet, and at the same time, tart lemon curd. Since the Minister of Desserts is purely fictitious, I can tell you that I often serve this tart in tandem with another dessert. Strawberries Poached in Cardamom-Scented Orange Juice (page 153) combines with the tart to make a heavenly union. For each serving, put the strawberries beside a slice of tart and drizzle the golden orange syrup over the tart.

For the pastry
   1 cup all-purpose flour
   $1/2$ teaspoon salt
   $1/2$ cup unsalted butter, cut into bits
   4 tablespoons ice water

For the lemon curd
   3 whole eggs
   3 egg yolks
   $1^1/4$ cups sugar
   Grated zest and juice of 2 lemons
   $1/2$ cup unsalted butter, cut into bits

1. Make the pastry: Combine the flour and salt in a bowl. Add the butter and toss. Cut the butter into the flour with a pastry blender or 2 knives until the mixture resembles oatmeal. Add the water, I tablespoon at a time, tossing with a fork until the pastry comes together. Form the pastry into a flattened ball,

wrap in plastic wrap or waxed paper, and chill for 20 minutes.

2. Make the lemon curd: In the top of a double boiler over low heat, beat the whole eggs. Beat in the egg yolks. Add the sugar and lemon zest and juice, whisking continuously until the mixture coats the back of a spoon. Remove from the heat and beat in the butter. Strain and bring to room temperature.

3. Preheat an oven to 350°F. On a lightly floured work surface, roll out the pastry into a circle large enough to cover the bottom and sides of a 9-inch fluted tart pan with removable sides. Press the pastry into the pan and trim away any excess. Prick the bottom and blind-bake (without weights) until the pastry is slightly golden, 15 minutes. Let cool on a rack.

4. Fill with the lemon curd. Chill thoroughly. Remove pan sides and serve.

Note: I like to make lemon curd whipped cream to serve with fresh fruit salad. Whip I cup of heavy cream until almost stiff. Using a rubber spatula, fold into I recipe of the lemon curd. It's not necessary to incorporate thoroughly; a swirled effect is appealing.

PUCCINI'S FAVORITE CHOCOLATE TART

Serves 16

As far as I know, there has never been a real opera house on Nantucket aside from the eponymous restaurant. However, the music of Puccini is the perfect accompaniment to dramatic Island evenings. I enjoy this tart, the specialty of the maestro's hometown of Lucca, while listening to any Puccini opera.

For the pastry
- 2$\frac{1}{4}$ cups all-purpose flour
- $\frac{1}{2}$ cup granulated sugar
- Pinch of salt
- $\frac{1}{2}$ cup plus 6 tablespoons unsalted butter
- 1 egg
- 1 teaspoon vanilla extract
- 1 tablespoon grated orange zest

For the filling
- 4 cups Dutch-process cocoa powder
- 2 cups confectioner's sugar
- $\frac{1}{2}$ cup granulated sugar
- $\frac{1}{4}$ teaspoon salt
- 1 cup strong coffee
- 1 cup milk
- $\frac{1}{2}$ cup plus 6 tablespoons unsalted butter
- 2 egg yolks

1. Make the pastry: Combine the flour, sugar, and salt in a food processor. Pulse several times. Cut and add the butter. Pulse until fully combined. Add the egg, vanilla, and orange zest. Pulse until the dough forms a ball on the blade. Divide the dough into two balls, one containing two-thirds of the dough and one containing one-third. Form into 2 balls, wrap in plastic wrap or waxed paper, and chill for 30 minutes.

2. Preheat an oven to 350°F. On a lightly floured work surface, roll out two-thirds of the dough into a circle large enough to cover the bottom and sides of a 10-inch fluted tart pan with removable sides. Press the pastry into the pan and trim any excess. Prick the bottom and blind-bake until the pastry is slightly golden, 15 to 20 minutes. Let cool on a rack.

3. Roll out the remaining dough to about $\frac{1}{8}$ inch thick. Cut into strips of varying lengths and widths. Place the strips, without touching, on a parchment paper–lined baking sheet and bake until golden, about 10 minutes. Let cool on a rack.

4. Make the filling: Sift together the cocoa, sugars, and salt. Combine the coffee, milk, and butter in a heavy-bottomed saucepan over medium heat. When the butter has melted, start stirring in the cocoa mixture, beating until smooth. Cook, stirring constantly, for 4 minutes, being careful not to let the mixture scorch on the pan bottom. Whisk in the egg yolks. Spoon the chocolate filling into the pastry shell and arrange the pastry strips over the top in a random pattern to make a "broken lattice." Chill for at least 2 hours.

5. Remove the tart from the refrigerator at least I hour before serving. Remove the pan sides and serve.

Note: This is an intensely rich tart, so you'll want to serve small pieces.

PEACH MELBA CROSTATA

Serves 8

To celebrate the divas of summer fruit—the raspberries that grow in profusion in many Nantucket backyards and the rosy-cheeked peaches piled in pyramids at the local supermarkets—I've put together this simple-to-make Peach Melba Crostata. Make this easy tart in the morning, put it on the windowsill to cool, go to the beach, and think about this: Chef Auguste Escoffier worshiped opera soprano Nellie Melba and in her honor created two distinct dishes. When she sang at Covent Garden, she stayed at London's grand Savoy Hotel, where Escoffier commanded the kitchen. For her diet-conscious breakfast, she requested dry toast made of bread sliced as thinly as possible. Escoffier prepared what has come to be known as melba toast, practically synonymous with diets. However, to celebrate her triumphant performance in Lohengrin, *her biggest fan created an equally splendid, but hardly dietetic dessert—vanilla ice cream topped with poached peaches, then covered with raspberry sauce.*

For the pastry

2¼ cups all-purpose flour

½ cup plus 1 tablespoon sugar

Pinch of salt

½ cup plus 6 tablespoons unsalted butter,
  cut into bits

2 eggs

1 teaspoon grated lemon zest

1 tablespoon cold water

For the filling

½ cup good-quality raspberry jam

¼ cup sugar

2½ cups peeled and sliced peaches

For the garnish

2 cups raspberries

1. Prepare the pastry: Combine the flour, ½ cup sugar, and salt in a food processor. Pulse several times. Add the butter and pulse until fully combined. Add I egg and the lemon zest. Pulse until the dough forms a ball on the blade. Divide in half, form into 2 balls, wrap in waxed paper or plastic wrap, and chill for at least 30 minutes.

2. Prepare the filling: In a nonreactive saucepan, mix the raspberry jam and sugar. Simmer until the sugar is completely dissolved. Add the peaches and cook over very low heat, just until slightly softened, 3 to 5 minutes depending on the degree of ripeness of the fruit. Let cool.

3. Preheat an oven to 350° F. Remove the pastry from the refrigerator and let come to room temperature, about 15 minutes. On a lightly floured work surface, roll out one of the pastry balls into a circle large enough to cover the bottom and sides of a 10-inch fluted tart pan with removable sides. Press the pastry into the pan and trim any excess. Prick the bottom. Fill with the raspberry-peach filling, spreading evenly with a rubber spatula.

4. Roll out the second pastry ball to the same size. Cut into strips ¾ inch wide. Arrange half of the strips, ½ inch apart, over the tart. Repeat with the remaining strips, placing them perpendicular to make a grid pattern. Trim any excess. There will be leftover pastry. I usually form another ball, roll it out, then cut out shapes such as circles, flowers, or hearts, and place them on top of the grid in a decorative way.

5. Make a wash by beating the remaining egg with the cold water in a small bowl. Brush the strips and decorations with the wash and sprinkle with the I tablespoon sugar. Bake until the top is golden, 30 to 35 minutes. Cool on a rack. Remove the pan sides. Serve each slice with a mound of fresh raspberries.

BLUEBERRIES ON NANTUCKET

Just as passionate clammers and scallopers in Nantucket have secret spots where they find their treasures, ardent blueberry pickers have equally hush-hush locations for their favorite fruit. While knowledge of these spots is stealthily passed down only within families, I can tell you that from late July through early August, wild blueberries can be found, in general, in two particular kinds of places.

Low-bush blueberries grow on the moors, where the plants thrive on the low-acid, rather poor soil. These berries are hard to find, nestled as they are among other low-growing heath vegetation. High-bush blueberries, on the other hand, grow in the fecund wetlands. Search for these famous Nantucket blueberries near the Island's many ponds and around the cranberry bog.

Cherish your personal blueberry harvest and please don't rinse them until just before you're ready to use them.

Puzzle Pudding, see pg. 146

GINGERY LIME-BLUEBERRY PIE

Serves 8

Good color, firm flesh, and plumpness tell you that it's time to pick the blueberries. Then make blueberry muffins, blueberry pancakes, blueberry preserves, and blueberry pie. These are the banner foods of summer in New England.

My irrepressible friend, Roy Finamore, whom I call His Royness for his elevated talents, took summer's sublime pie a few steps further and created this tangy, spicy, and very blueberry pie. I love to serve it floating on heavy cream.

For the pastry

2¹⁄₂ **cups sifted all-purpose flour**

2 **tablespoons sugar**

¹⁄₄ **teaspoon salt**

¹⁄₂ **cup chilled vegetable shortening, cut into bits**

¹⁄₂ **cup unsalted butter, cut into bits**

4 **to 6 tablespoons ice water**

For the filling

1¹⁄₂ **cups sugar**

¹⁄₄ **cup cornstarch**

¹⁄₂ **teaspoon ground cinnamon**

Freshly ground white pepper

5 **cups blueberries**

2 **tablespoons mild-flavored honey**

Juice of 1 lime

¹⁄₂ **teaspoon grated fresh ginger**

1. Make the pastry: Combine the flour, I tablespoon of the sugar, and salt in a bowl. Add the shortening and toss. Add the butter and toss. Cut the fats into the flour with a pastry blender or 2 knives until the mixture resembles oatmeal. Add the water, I or 2 tablespoons at a time, tossing with a fork until the pastry comes together. Knead 2 or 3 times on a lightly floured work surface. Divide the pastry in half, form into 2 flattened balls, wrap in plastic wrap or waxed paper, and refrigerate for 30 minutes.

2. Make the filling: Combine the sugar, cornstarch, cinnamon, and 3 or 4 twists of pepper in a bowl. Put the berries in another bowl and toss with the honey, lime juice, and ginger.

3. Preheat the oven to 450°F. Butter a 9¹⁄₂-inch glass pie dish. On a lightly floured work surface, roll out I pastry disk into a circle large enough to cover the bottom and sides of the prepared pie dish. Sprinkle one-third of the sugar mixture over the bottom of the pastry. Add the remaining sugar mixture to the berries and toss gently. Spoon the berries into the pastry.

4. Roll out the remaining pastry into a circle large enough to cover the berries. Trim the overlap to ¹⁄₂ inch, fold under, and crimp. Sprinkle with the remaining I tablespoon sugar. Bake for 20 minutes. Reduce heat to 350°F and bake until the pastry is browned and the juices bubbling, 45 minutes. Cool on a rack and serve.

PUZZLE PUDDING

Serves 6

Hazel Mellin's sons, one of whom owns "Airdrie," the cottage I rent every summer, remember their Nantucket summers in the late 1920s well. There was a clear view from the house to the ocean, and the great sport was to watch the Coast Guard cutters chasing the rumrunners in the water just off Squam's shores. This ranked right up there with picking blueberries and fishing in the pond. The results of those two activities would be transformed as if by magic into delightful dinners. Dinah Mellin, the wife of Hazel's grandson John, shared some of grandma's recipes with me. This is an update of her pudding, an ideal dessert for a summer supper and an even better breakfast the next morning.

2 large eggs

2 cups buttermilk

$\frac{1}{2}$ cup sugar

1 teaspoon vanilla extract

1 cup all-purpose flour

1 teaspoon baking powder

2 cups blueberries

$1\frac{1}{2}$ cups raspberries

$\frac{3}{4}$ cup firmly packed dark brown sugar
   for the garnish

1 cup heavy cream

$1\frac{1}{2}$ cups sliced strawberries

1. Preheat an oven to 350°F. In a bowl, whisk together the eggs, buttermilk, sugar, and vanilla until well blended. Sift together the flour and baking powder. Add to the liquid, a bit at a time, whisking until smooth after each addition.

2. Generously butter a $9\frac{1}{2}$-by-11-inch baking dish or a gratin dish. Distribute the berries evenly in the dish. Pour the batter over the fruit. Sprinkle the brown sugar over the top.

3. Bake until the batter is set, at least 1 hour. Some of the berries will rise to the top, forming puzzlelike patterns with the batter and brown sugar. Serve cool, which brings out the flavor of the individual fruits. Place each serving on a puddle of heavy cream, and cover with a cascade of strawberries.

RICHARD SAX'S CORNMEAL CAKE WITH POACHED SUMMER FRUITS

Serves 8 to 10

On September 1, 1995, a few friends and I were sitting outside my cottage, "Airdrie," watching a spectacular sunset and enjoying a cocktail, when the news of Richard Sax's death reached us. Brillat-Savarin said something like in order to be a good cook you have to have a big heart. In the food world no one has ever had a heart bigger than Richard Sax. With an uncommonly generous spirit, he shared information and recipes, and patiently listened to complaints and panic attacks from less experienced authors. Roy Finamore was there that sad September evening. To celebrate the memory of a dear friend, he adapted one of Richard's cornmeal cake recipes from his masterwork, Classic Home Desserts *(Chapters Publishing, 1994), for this book.*

For the cake

- 1 cup stone-ground cornmeal, plus cornmeal for dusting
- 1/2 cup sifted all-purpose flour
- 1 1/2 teaspoons baking powder
- 1/4 teaspoon salt
- 1 cup unsalted butter
- 1 cup sugar
- 4 eggs
- 1/4 cup sour cream
- Grated zest and juice of 1 lemon
- 1/2 teaspoon lemon extract

For the fruit

- 1 bottle (750 milliliters) red wine
- 2 cups sugar
- 2 pieces of orange zest, about 3 inches long
- 1 cinnamon stick, about 2 inches long
- 1 teaspoon allspice berries
- 1/2 teaspoon coriander seeds
- 3 or 4 white peppercorns
- 4 pounds assorted fruits such as plums, nectarines, and cherries (see Note)
- 2 tablespoons crème de cassis

1. Make the cake: Preheat an oven to 375°F. Butter a 9- or 10-inch round cake pan and dust well with cornmeal. Sift together the cornmeal, flour, baking powder, and salt.

2. In a large bowl, beat the butter until light. Add the sugar and beat until light and fluffy, about 5 minutes. Beat in the eggs, one at a time. Stir in the sour cream, lemon zest and juice, and lemon extract. The mixture will look curdled. Add the flour mixture and fully incorporate by carefully folding with a rubber spatula.

3. Spoon the batter into the prepared pan, even out the top, and bake until golden and firm, about 50 minutes. Cool thoroughly on a rack, then turn out onto a cake plate.

4. Make the fruit: Combine the wine and sugar in a nonreactive saucepan over medium heat. Stir to dissolve the sugar. Place the orange zest, cinnamon, allspice, coriander, and peppercorns on a piece of cheesecloth and tie together to make a bag. Add to the wine and simmer for 10 minutes.

5. Poach each kind of fruit separately in the liquid until tender. Remove the fruit with a slotted spoon or a skimmer, and reserve in a bowl. Raise the heat to high and cook the poaching liquid until reduced to about I cup, about I hour. Remove the spice bundle. Stir in the cassis.

6. Spoon some of the syrup over the cake and the remainder over the fruit. Serve the sliced cake with the fruit on top of it or alongside it.

Note: I used 4 pounds of plums, nectarines, and cherries for this recipe. However, the syrup will take up to 10 pounds of fruit. As you add extra fruit, it releases its juice, thus increasing the liquid. If you're feeling energetic, poach some extra fruit. It will last for several weeks in the refrigerator. After the cake is long gone, poached summer fruits with vanilla ice cream make an easy and impressive dessert.

HOT CHOCOLATE LOGS

Makes 3 dozen logs

Chocolate, which is basically cacao mixed with sugar, has always contained other ingredients that combine to give it its final flavor. The most popularly added flavor is vanilla, which the Aztecs, the world's first chocolatiers, used to enhance the taste. The native Mexicans also pounded cacao beans together with ingredients such as honey, hot peppers, black pepper, cloves, and cinnamon to form a paste. Hot water and the paste became a satisfying drink that would eventually conquer the courts of Europe. Sometime in the eighteenth century, the English added milk to the chocolate to make the drink that we know and love so much today.

I like what chocolate does when blended with punchy spices like cinnamon and black pepper. I especially like a cookie jar filled with these Hot Chocolate Logs during Nantucket's languid summer months when the living is easy. After a day at the beach, dessert is as simple as stopping at a farm stand for watermelon, then cutting it into triangles and arranging it decoratively with a stack of chocolate logs.

$\frac{1}{2}$ cup unsalted butter

$\frac{1}{2}$ cup firmly packed dark brown sugar

1 egg

$\frac{1}{2}$ teaspoon vanilla extract

$1\frac{1}{4}$ cups all-purpose flour

$1\frac{1}{2}$ tablespoons cocoa powder

$\frac{1}{4}$ teaspoon baking powder

1 tablespoon ground cinnamon

$\frac{3}{4}$ teaspoon salt

$\frac{3}{4}$ cup semisweet chocolate pieces

$\frac{1}{2}$ teaspoon freshly ground black pepper

For the glaze

$\frac{1}{4}$ cup milk

2 tablespoons confectioner's sugar

$\frac{1}{2}$ teaspoon ground cinnamon

1. Preheat an oven to 350°F. In a large bowl, cream together the butter and sugar. Add the egg and vanilla. Sift together the flour, cocoa powder, baking powder, cinnamon, and salt. Add to the butter mixture. Add the chocolate pieces and black pepper.

2. Spread the batter evenly in a 9- by 12-inch baking pan with 1-inch sides. Bake until the batter is set and smooth, about 20 minutes.

3. Make the glaze: Put the milk in a small saucepan over low heat. Add the sugar and cinnamon, and stir to dissolve the sugar.

4. Remove the baking pan from the oven after 20 minutes and brush the glaze over the entire surface once or twice. Return to the oven for 3 to 4 minutes.

5. Cool on a rack. First cut into 12 pieces, 3 on the short side by 4 on the long side. Then cut each piece into 3 logs.

MAIN STREET COBBLES CRANBERRY-APPLE COBBLER

Serves 6 to 8

The Native Americans of Massachusetts, who "invented" cranberry sauce, used the berry for medicinal purposes as much as for food. While this cobbler, named for Nantucket's ever-present cobblestones, isn't really a medicine, every mouthful is guaranteed to make you feel better. I strongly suggest that you serve it with Maple Syrup Crème Anglaise (page 128).

For the fruit

- 1 orange
- 1 cup sugar
- 1 cup cranberries
- 4 large Mutsu or Granny Smith apples, peeled, cored, and cut into chunks
- 1/2 teaspoon ground cinnamon
- Pinch of ground allspice
- 2 tablespoons unsalted butter

For the biscuits

- 2 cups all-purpose flour
- 2 tablespoons sugar
- 3 teaspoons baking powder
- 1/2 teaspoon baking soda
- Pinch of salt
- 6 tablespoons unsalted butter, cut into bits and chilled
- 1 cup buttermilk, plus buttermilk for brushing
- 1/2 cup slivered almonds

1. Preheat an oven to 350° F. Lightly butter an 8-cup low-sided baking dish.

2. Prepare the fruit: Remove the zest from half the orange using a vegetable peeler and place in a food processor. Juice half the orange and set aside. Save the rest of the orange for another use. Add the sugar to the zest and process until the zest is very finely minced and the sugar is orange colored. Transfer to a mixing bowl. Put the cranberries in the food processor and pulse until coarsely chopped. Transfer to the bowl with the sugar. Add the apples, orange juice, cinnamon, and allspice. Toss well and turn into the prepared baking dish. Dot with the 2 tablespoons butter.

3. Prepare the biscuits: Combine the flour, sugar, baking powder, baking soda, and salt in a bowl. Add the butter and toss. Cut the butter into the flour mixture with a pastry blender or 2 knives until the mixture resembles coarse cornmeal. Add the 1 cup buttermilk and toss with a fork until the dough starts to come together.

4. Turn the dough out onto a floured work surface and knead lightly and quickly until smooth. Pat the dough with floured hands to about 1/2 inch thick, and cut out rounds with a 2-inch-diameter biscuit cutter. Place the biscuits, sides touching, over the fruit. Gently press the scraps together, knead again, and cut out more biscuits; you will probably need to use all the dough to cover the fruit. Brush the biscuits with buttermilk and scatter with the almonds.

5. Bake the cobbler until the biscuits are nicely browned and the fruit is bubbling, about 45 minutes. Cool on a rack. Serve warm or at room temperature.

STRAWBERRIES POACHED IN CARDAMOM-SCENTED ORANGE JUICE

Serves 6

In Nantucket, strawberries are the month of June's most popular crop. Though slow to arrive, they finish quickly. Fresh local strawberries, ripened on the vine, are a treat—they are sweet and succulent. Sometimes when the berries are still plentiful, you can go out to a farm and pick your own. Load up on them while they're available. Freeze some to make a surprise New Year's strawberry shortcake.

1 cup orange juice

1 cup dry white vermouth or spicy white wine such as sauvignon blanc

½ cup sugar

6 cardamom pods

3 cups strawberries, hulled

1. In a saucepan, bring all the ingredients, except the strawberries, to a boil. Immediately reduce the heat and simmer for 10 minutes.

2. Add the strawberries and poach for 90 seconds. Remove from the poaching liquid and let cool. Remove and discard the cardamom pods. Cook the liquid over low heat until reduced to a syrup. This should take 30 to 45 minutes.

3. Serve at room temperature or chilled.

B

CHAPTER SEVEN

EVERAGES

The Opera House

From 1946 to 1986, Gwen and Harold Gaillard ran the Opera House restaurant on Nantucket. It was the quintessential summer restaurant, with an insouciance made possible by Gwen's eclectic taste. Her decor of Victorian and turn-of-the-century collectibles gave the Opera House its ambiance and its name. Gwen's determination to offer food that contrasted with the fancy selections at local hotels gave the restaurant its first-class, no-nonsense menu—and spawned establishments with a similar style.

The great bar, frequented by locals, fancy summer people, and swaggering sailors, served delicious and bountiful drinks. When the restaurant hosted a party, Gwen would bring out her huge silver punch bowl and make a potent concoction called Bombay Cooler. She says that this punch put most of Nantucket out of commission for at least one day following the party—gas stations closed and electricians never showed up for appointments. Clients who had one or two drinks too many were personally escorted home by Gwen, and their cars were returned by the stalwart Opera House waiters.

Bombay Cooler

Serves 36

The recipe for this colorful and powerful punch was graciously given to me by Gwen Gaillard. It's from her classic collection, Recipes with Love, *published in 1966 on Nantucket. For Gwen, who always provided a party for all who entered her restaurant and her home, lift a glass of this tasty punch to toast good times. Gwen requests that no substitutes be used in this recipe.*

- 1 large block ice
- 1 bottle (750 milliliters) cognac or good brandy
- ½ bottle (375 milliliters) good-quality dry sherry
- 1 cup Cointreau or Triple Sec
- ½ cup maraschino liqueur
- 4 cups sparkling water
- 3 bottles (750 milliliters each) champagne
- 1 large bunch champagne grapes or red seedless grapes

1. Place a large block of ice in an extra-large punch bowl. Pour the cognac or brandy, sherry, Cointreau or Triple Sec, maraschino liqueur, and sparkling water over the ice. Add the champagne. Place the grapes on top of the ice as a garnish. Ladle into pretty stemmed glasses to serve.

TOM ECKERLE'S MINTIEST MINT JULEP

Serves 6

Tom Eckerle, who took the glorious photographs for this book, is a bon vivant in every sense of the word. I'm convinced that his passion for the daily rituals involving food and drink led him to specialize in food photography. In Tom's life, dinner always begins after a drink and a rehashing of the events of the day. The cocktail is enjoyed as much for its taste as for its preparation. With much practice Tom has created the ultimate mint julep. It is a very strong drink, so sip it slowly!

1 cup firmly packed fresh mint leaves, plus 18 sprigs for garnish
$^1/_2$ cup superfine sugar
$2^1/_4$ cups fine Kentucky bourbon
4 pounds shaved ice (see Note)

1. In an electric herb chopper or a mini food processor, process the 1 cup mint leaves and the sugar until finely chopped. Put $1^1/_2$ tablespoons of the mint-sugar mixture into each of 6 silver mint julep cups or collins glasses. Add 6 tablespoons of bourbon to each cup or glass and swirl to combine. Place in the freezer for 10 minutes.

2. Remove the cups or glasses from the freezer and fill each one to the brim with shaved ice. Place a long, sturdy straw in each. Trim the stems from the mint sprigs and immediately place in each beverage as a garnish.

Note: Ice cubes can be made into shaved ice by processing 1 pound at a time in a food processor.

TIEPOLO

Serves 5 or 6

Named for the eighteenth-century Venetian painter, the Tiepolo is made with summer's first strawberries and is as fragrant and refreshing as a walk in the June woods. Created at Venice's fabled Café Florian in Piazza San Marco, this aperitif features prosecco, the very dry, tiny-bubbled white wine of the Veneto region and a purée of strawberries. It was created in an attempt, no doubt, to compete with the extraordinarily well-known Bellini, made with prosecco and peach nectar, which was served at neighboring Harry's Bar.

The beautiful blue-and-white porcelain bowl used to chill the glasses is called a Monteith. Invented in England in the late seventeenth century (just as Tiepolo was born), this receptacle is used specifically to hold ice water for rinsing and chilling wineglasses. Lord Monteith's bar accessory was probably made in a factory in China and transported to our shores by a Nantucket merchant ship. Nantucket's association with the China trade is not nearly as well known as the whaling industry—but was certainly as successful.

2 cups strawberries
1 bottle (750 milliliters) ice-cold prosecco or very dry champagne

1. Save 5 or 6 perfect strawberries for a garnish. Remove the hulls from the remainder and purée in a food processor. Place 1 tablespoon of the strawberry purée in each glass. A champagne flute works well. Gently stir the purée as you pour the prosecco into the glass.

Note: The purée can also be frozen for later use.

THE AIRDRIE

Serves 1

This drink is named for the little cottage that I live in every summer. The peace of mind and well-being that I experience while at "Airdrie" probably deserve more than just a drink named for it. However, this cocktail is an ambrosial reminder of one of my favorite places on earth. How can you argue with that?

6 tablespoons vodka
1 tablespoon fresh orange juice
1 teaspoon crème de cassis
½ orange slice

1. Fill an old-fashioned glass with ice. Pour the vodka over the ice. Add the orange juice and stir. Add the cassis, and let it float around the glass. Slip the orange slice down the side of the glass and serve.

BARLEY WATER LEMONADE

Serves 6

No other drink is more synonymous with summer than lemonade. Aside from its obvious thirst-quenching qualities, lemonade reminds us of our very first money-making venture, the lemonade stand. The lemonade stand has a historical precedent dating back to the early 1830s. During the temperance movement, which was spearheaded in 1827 by the American Society for the Promotion of Temperance in Boston, lemonade was offered as a lively alternative to alcohol. It became the drink of choice when it was sold from stands at special events such as agricultural expositions and ladies' charitable fairs—and at Nantucket's annual Sheep Shearing Day festival.

The Victorians, who were extremely concerned with their physical well-being, used barley water, a well-known kidney cleanser, as the base for lemonade and created a healthy and refreshing drink.

½ cup pearl barley, rinsed and drained

8 cups water

3 large lemons

½ cup superfine sugar

Optional: fresh lemon balm or mint leaves
   for garnish

1. In a heavy-bottomed, nonreactive saucepan, combine the barley and the water. Peel the zest from 2 of the lemons with a vegetable peeler. Add the zest to the barley and simmer, covered, for 2 hours.

2. Juice all 3 lemons into a small bowl. Add the sugar and stir vigorously to combine.

3. Working over a pitcher, drain the barley from the water. Add the sweetened lemon juice to the barley water in the pitcher. Stir to combine. Chill before serving. Serve in tall glasses with lots of ice. Garnish with lemon balm or mint leaves, if desired.

Note: This recipe makes a very strong, lemony drink. You may want to thin it with more water or seltzer.

HONEY-MINT ICED TEA

Serves 8

Introduced for the first time at the St. Louis World's Fair in 1904, iced tea is clearly an American invention. The rest of the tea-drinking world looks down their noses at the very idea of chilling a beverage that has always been served hot. No matter, on a hot summer day, I'd rather have a glass of iced tea than any other drink.

This is my Nantucket iced tea. I always make it with honey from Jimmy's apiary and fresh mint from Laura's garden. I like to season the whole pitcher of tea at a time. This way I'm assured that my last glass of tea will taste like my first.

6 cups water

4 tea bags, preferably black tea such as Assam, Darjeeling, or Lapsang Souchong

2 rounded tablespoons pure honey

Juice of 1 lemon

20 fresh mint sprigs

1. Bring the water to a boil in a saucepan. Place the tea bags, honey, lemon juice, and mint into a pitcher. I usually tie the tea bags to the pitcher's handle so they can hang into the pitcher without getting lost. Pour the boiling water into the pitcher. Stir a few minutes to combine. Let cool. Serve in tall glasses with lots of ice.

ATHENEUM PUNCH

Serves 20

One cloudless August afternoon not too long ago, a party was held in the garden of the Nantucket Atheneum. The event was to celebrate the end of the children's summer reading program, "Sail on a Sea of Books." Margaret MacElderry, longtime Nantucket summer resident and the doyenne of children's book publishers, was the honored guest. This was a special occasion and it deserved significant snacks. A white-clothed table was placed in the protective shade of the garden's venerable trees, and my friend Gillie and I proceeded to load it with baskets of cookies, trays of strawberry-and-cream-cheese sandwiches, and a huge bowl of this punch created especially for the festivities.

2 pounds crushed ice

4 cups chilled orange juice

4 cups chilled cranberry juice

1 bottle (1 liter) chilled ginger ale

1 bottle (1 liter) chilled seltzer

2 oranges, sliced

2 cups strawberries, sliced

$\frac{1}{2}$ cup loosely packed fresh mint leaves

1. Place the crushed ice in a large punch bowl. Pour the fruit juices, ginger ale, and seltzer over the ice. Cut the orange slices into quarters and add to the punch. Add the strawberries and gently swirl. Float the mint leaves on top. Serve immediately.

SPICY CRANBERRY JUICE

Serves 8

One of my most enduring memories of my family's trips to Nantucket in the early years was taking the Cranberry Highway to one of the two bridges that crossed the Cape Cod Canal. The landmark that I eagerly looked forward to was the Ocean Spray Cranberry factory. I was excited to be so close to the factory that made the cranberry jelly that shimmered out of its can to sit beside our Thanksgiving turkey.

Since those summer trips, the Ocean Spray label, which today appears on lots of products, is a visual souvenir of happy times. I'm sure that Ocean Spray, which buys just about all of Nantucket's cranberries for its products, won't mind if I tell you how to make this spicy and festive cranberry juice.

1 pound cranberries

1 cup sugar

2 cinnamon sticks, about 2 inches long

1 teaspoon whole cloves

1 teaspoon cardamom pods

6 cups water

1 orange, sliced

1 lemon, sliced

1. In a heavy-bottomed, nonreactive saucepan, combine the cranberries, sugar, cinnamon sticks, cloves, and cardamom with the water. Simmer, with the cover askew, for 45 minutes. Let cool. Strain the juice into a pitcher or jar. Chill before serving.

2. Pour over lots of ice to serve. Garnish each glass with orange and lemon slices.

Note: This juice works well with rum to make a robust cocktail.

INDEX

TABLE OF EQUIVALENTS

The exact equivalents in the following tables have been rounded for convenience.

LIQUID AND DRY MEASURES

U.S.	METRIC
$\frac{1}{4}$ teaspoon	1.25 milliliters
$\frac{1}{2}$ teaspoon	2.5 milliliters
1 teaspoon	5 milliliters
1 tablespoon (3 teaspoons)	15 milliliters
1 fluid ounce (2 tablespoons)	30 milliliters
$\frac{1}{4}$ cup	60 milliliters
$\frac{1}{3}$ cup	80 milliliters
1 cup	240 milliliters
1 pint (2 cups)	480 milliliters
1 quart (4 cups, 32 ounces)	960 milliliters
1 gallon (4 quarts)	3.84 liters
1 ounce (by weight)	28 grams
$\frac{1}{4}$ pound (4 ounces)	114 grams
1 pound	454 grams
2.2 pounds	1 kilogram

LENGTH MEASURES

U.S.	METRIC
$\frac{1}{8}$ inch	3 millimeters
$\frac{1}{4}$ inch	6 millimeters
$\frac{1}{2}$ inch	12 millimeters
1 inch	2.5 centimeters

OVEN TEMPERATURES

FAHRENHEIT	CELSIUS	GAS
250	120	$\frac{1}{2}$
275	140	1
300	150	2
325	160	3
350	180	4
375	190	5
400	200	6
425	220	7
450	230	8
475	240	9
500	260	10